YORKSHIRE
CRICKET
GREATS

YORKSHIRE
CRICKET
GREATS

John Callaghan

SPORTSPRINT PUBLISHING
EDINBURGH

© John Callaghan 1990

All rights reserved.

No part of this publication may be reproduced
in any form or by any means without
the prior permission of the publishers,
John Donald Publishers Ltd.,
138 St Stephen Street, Edinburgh EH3 5AA

ISBN 0 85976 325 0

British Library Cataloguing in Publication Data
Callaghan, John *1938-*
  Yorkshire cricket greats.
  1. Cricketers, history
  I. Title
  796.3580922

Phototypeset by Beecee Typesetting Services
Printed and bound in Great Britain by Charles Letts (Scotland) Ltd

ACKNOWLEDGEMENTS

This is not a book of great research. The intention has been to show the man behind the deeds, and a few facts and figures are given for those who like them. The background information has been gained down the years through informal talks with the people concerned, and I am grateful for the many hours they have spent with me in various parts of the country. The cricket circuit is, in many ways, rather like a family. I must also thank the editor of the *Yorkshire Evening Post* for kindly allowing access to the files and for permission to use a selection of pictures.

J.C.

C O N T E N T S

The Yorkshire team of 1968, when the county last won the championship, included (left to right): back row — John Hampshire, Tony Nicholson, Richard Hutton, Don Wilson, Doug Padgett, Phil Sharpe; front — Jimmy Binks, Fred Trueman, Brian Close, Ray Illingworth, Ken Taylor.

INTRODUCTION

Yorkshire have achieved a pre-eminence in cricket which is unequalled in any other form of sporting endeavour, although it has not been easy to accept that fact during the turbulent days of the past twenty years. The facts, however, are clear. Despite their endless internal squabbles and two barren decades, the county can still boast an outstanding record which remains out of the reach of the newcomers to honours. The only true test of ability in domestic cricket is the championship, which Yorkshire have won thirty times since 1890, when it was official organised, including one occasion upon which they had to share the ultimate prize. The other sixteen first-class counties line up in a respectful queue, the list reading: Surrey sixteen championships, Middlesex ten, Lancashire eight, Kent seven, Worcestershire five, Essex and Nottinghamshire four, Warwickshire three, Glamorgan and Hampshire two, Derbyshire and Leicestershire one. Gloucestershire, Northamptonshire, Somerset, even with Ian Botham and Viv Richards, and Sussex have still to register their first success.

Taking into account the various one-day competitions, Yorkshire are one of only four counties to win all four major trophies, Essex, Kent and Lancashire being the others. Even so, the post-war period has been disappointing, although bringing nine championships, two Gillette Cups, one Benson and Hedges Trophy and one Sunday League title — a catalogue of success which their rivals might well envy. The trouble is that Yorkshire's proud tradition has become something of a millstone around the neck of the modern players.

Many have come to resent not only the great deeds of the past, but also the public obsession with them, feeling that whatever they do they will never be recognised in their own right. They, probably more than the membership, are aware that things have changed. Before the second world war, many first-class counties had no ambition beyond surviving for another season. Their teams were patched up with amateurs, who cost little or nothing, and there is an element of truth in the stories of the hard-headed Yorkshire players booking accommodation, for which they had to pay themselves, for only two nights, working on the theory that they were unlikely to need a bed for the third.

To a large extent, Yorkshire's decline has contrasted with a general, all-round improvement in the standards of the other first-class counties, brought about by the mass influx of overseas Test stars. Indeed, dressing-room concern at the imbalance became so acute that an approach was made to the committee by captain Phil Carrick in 1989, suggesting that outside aid should be sought. Inevitably, the implied admission that Yorkshire cricket could no longer stand squarely on its own feet brought an angry response from the membership, who jealously guarded their tradition, conveniently overlooking the fact that at least twenty-nine men born outside the Broad Acres have represented Yorkshire.

There is, though, rather more to Yorkshire's problems than a mere shift in the balance of power and the continuing successes of their under-16 and under-19 teams confirm the proud boast that the county still produce more than their share of above-average talent.

The question mark curls interestingly around the inability of the once almost infallible Yorkshire system to transform potential into highly polished performance. To a large extent the committee are to blame, for they have presided over a failing club without coming to terms with the realities of a steadily worsening situation. The faces have changed, but the pattern has remained the same. Safely sheltered by the barricades of privilege, the committee have been out of touch with both the membership and the dressing room.

Clinging grimly to an outdated system, they have steadfastly set the collective face of the administration against change. Twenty-three representatives cover seventeen districts under a complicated and totally unfair arrangement. Leeds, Sheffield and Bradford, as the major areas of population, elect three men to the committee, while each of the other geographical divisions is limited to one voice. It is a long-standing set-up which has no statistical justification in the 1990s. Sheffield, for example, had only 640 members in 1989, while North Riding and York had 731 and 795 respectively. The situation led to the feeling that local interests were sometimes put first.

The county club, spreading their fixtures as widely as possible, continue to pay ground rental to play at Harrogate, Sheffield, Hull, Middlesbrough and Scarborough, which makes little financial sense as they are committed to the same costs at Headingley whether they play one match or ten at headquarters.

Within the framework of the committee structure, there are cricket, finance, grounds and membership and public relations and fund-raising sub-committees, with the chairmen sitting on the powerful management committee alongside the general committee chairman, the president and the treasurer. Not surprisingly the division of power within the committee is challenged on a regular basis, either openly or in quiet groups, and Viscount Mountgarret refused to accept renomination to the presidency in 1990 as a figurehead. He had taken an active role in the club's affairs and clearly upset some committee men. In the winter of 1981-82 the club subjected itself to a searching self-analysis with a sub-committee being formed under an independent chairman to investigate all aspects of the county's operation.

Among the recommendations of this body, who consulted all manner of opinion, was the 'reduction in the size of the decision-taking body within the committee.' The management committee represented a step in that direction, yet the full committee fought to retain overall power and the object of the exercise was lost. It was further suggested that a chief executive be appointed, but, in order to keep control, the committee put that particular idea on the 'back burner' and turned off the gas. They did the same with the recommendation that a commercial manager be appointed. In consequence, things were much the same in 1990 as they had been in 1980 with Yorkshire cricket going in no particular direction.

The committee appointed and sacked one manager in Ray Illingworth and turned to another, Steve Oldham, seven years later. The cricket sub-committee defiantly held on to office, however, so that yet again authority had to be shared.

The treatment of Geoff Boycott illustrated the extent of official confusion. Having been awarded a testimonial for 1984, he was sacked as a player. To the man in the street this did not make sense, nor did a subsequent attempt to take the heat out of a deteriorating situation. The committee actually put forward a compromise which would have involved Boycott playing in one match on each of the five home grounds irrespective of individual form or any other consideration. It was the sort of policy-making which eventually turned many moderates against the administration. The very idea of Boycott slipping in and out of the first team on the basis of a predetermined pattern flew in the face of logic — as most people readily recognised — and it never came to anything.

In the circumstances, it was not perhaps surprising that Yorkshire cricket continued to lack a collective sense of purpose. The tendency to look for excuses remained and the lack of success on the field kept the spotlight on the bitter in-fighting.

When, in the middle of the apparently endless rows over Boycott in the 1970s and '80s it became fashionable to talk glibly about that great intangible 'team-spirit', one senior ex-player quietly observed: 'They should have spent a few minutes in the dressing room in my day. It was like living in a nest of vipers.' Brian Bolus departed for Nottinghamshire and a seven-Test spell in the England side in 1962, having publicly criticised the administration, complaining of inequality of opportunity. In isolation, his views might have been dismissed, yet there was plenty of support for this popular, easy going batsman's outspoken comments.

The sensational sacking of left-arm spinner Johnny Wardle in 1958 had already revealed some of the rocks lurking below the apparently tranquil waters, and there were other problem areas. It was, for example, apparently only an accident of timing in the announcing of his retirement which denied Fred Trueman the Yorkshire captaincy in 1969.

In his autobiography, *Ball of Fire*, Trueman wrote that, having made the decision to turn his attention to other things, he had a personal interview with Sir William Worsley, then Yorkshire's president. Sir William, says Trueman, informed him that a meeting was to be held in the following week after which he would probably be offered the captaincy. 'I told Sir William that if someone had only hinted about the possibility I would have been delighted to play on for another two or three years,' Trueman added. Trueman's interview with Sir William must have been in the November of 1968, which is when he announced his intention to give up cricket, although the county had completed a wholly satisfactory season. For the third year in succession they were county champions and the annual report subsequently paid tribute to 'inspiring leadership' by Brian Close. Still, no one appears ever to have challenged the accuracy of Trueman's recollections. If we take his words at face value, we must assume that there had been plotting behind the scenes to get rid of Close, who eventually went in far from satisfactory circumstances two years later.

Illingworth was also lost to Yorkshire in 1968, allowed to go when at the height of his powers, not only as a much-respected all-rounder but also as a master tactician. By the time that Boycott took over the leadership, the club found itself desperately short of experience and professionalism. The county's ongoing strength was based on the continual handing down of knowledge, with standards being maintained by the iron rule of the senior professionals. The amateur captains, after imposing a sense of discipline, left much to the men who knew far more about the game than they did. Thus Emmott Robinson, a legendary folk hero of the 1920s, took the emerging Bill Bowes under his wing. He instructed Bowes, an embryonic pace bowler, to buy a penny notebook and a pencil and write down carefully at the end of each day all that he had learned. 'It was money well spent,' Bowes said. 'That little book stayed with me for years and came in useful time and time again when I wanted to recall something about a player on the other side.'

Even as England bowlers, Bowes and the very great left-arm spinner Hedley Verity had to spend time in the evenings after play listening to Wilfred Rhodes. Praise did not come easily or regularly and, more often than not, the statistically most successful of all English cricketers offered some suggestion as to how they might improve. Again Bowes readily appreciated the value of the exercise. 'Hedley and I never got careless about our cricket, even in the years when we regularly headed the national averages and Yorkshire were carrying all before them. Always we looked to do better and we knew that any slackness would be immediately noticed and brought to our attention in no uncertain terms.' Players saw nothing wrong in spending their spare time in talking and thinking about cricket, but gradually that sort of intense involvement turned into a chore.

As the strong, successful side of the late 1960s broke up, things were allowed to drift. Senior members of the staff went to the committee behind Boycott's back to complain about his captaincy and were pacified. The cricket chairman, John Temple, a man lacking the stature of Brian Sellers, the former captain from when he took over, exercised no real authority and little influence over the dressing room. Yorkshire's policy was a recipe for inevitable disaster.

Tony Nicholson, a high-quality seam bowler between 1962 and 1975, drew attention to the serious state of affairs casually when acting as twelfth man in his final season. Having endured some 'lip' from several junior members of the team, he observed, 'The trouble with Yorkshire cricket is that there is no discipline. When I first got into the side I never throught of speaking until someone spoke to me. I was literally terrified of the senior professionals. Now kids come into the team, get a few runs or a handful of wickets and they reckon they know everything. Say anything to them and you get back fifty words for one. Unless something is done damn quick, the club will go down the drain.'

He was, of course, right. The committee set the tone and everyone else grew to believe the long standing traditions were old-fashioned. It was much too easy to blame Boycott for just about everything from poor results to the shortage of soap in the ladies' powder room.

The committee also found it convenient to excuse their own shortcomings by referring to a shortage of talent, suggesting that the leagues no longer fulfilled their time-honoured functions of discovering and developing players. In that area, too, they missed the mark and overlooked the facts.

Throughout the barren period of the 1970s and '80s, a number of very promising youngsters emerged from the pipeline. Richard Lumb, Peter Squires, Bill Athey, Kevin Sharp, Jim Love, Martyn Moxon, Paul Javis, Arnie Sidebottom and Ashley Metcalfe all looked the part at one time or another and several of them went on to play for England at some level, but somehow something has always been missing.

This is particularly the case with Graham Stevenson, whose two Test 'caps' represent an inadequate reflection of his undoubted brilliance. Stevenson burst onto the scene at much same time as Ian Botham — 1973 against 1974 — and, while it may seem a foolish idea now, he was regarded in several quarters as the better prospect. Illingworth, not given to wild flights of fancy, says without hesitation: 'I have never seen any player in my life who could walk out to the middle and hit the first ball he received so far with such instinctive timing.'

Stevenson, without any noticeable effort, could do just about anything. He bowled a lively medium pace and made the ball move sharply, he maintained casual mastery of every stroke in the coaching manual, achieving the highest unbeaten score by a number eleven batsman in first-class cricket when he contributed 115 to a county record last-wicket partnership of 149 with Boycott against Warwickshire at Edgbaston in 1982. He also possessed a fine arm in the outfield and a reliable pair of hands. All he required to become a great cricketer was application. It was never going to be easy to put an old.head on his shoulders, yet the feeling persists that Yorkshire in general and the cricket committee in particular betrayed his potential and their office by allowing him to waste his career. After the big Edgbaston partnership, Boycott pointed out: 'It was all down to my brains and Graham's ability.'

Inevitably, his remark attracted criticism, yet he was merely stating the obvious. Stevenson on that occasion played with unexpected restraint, selecting his strokes carefully and avoiding any foolish error, constantly being advised by his partner. Had Yorkshire's committee paid similar attention to the details of his development they might easily have created a great player. Certainly they had a duty to try a lot harder than they did, a point that applies equally to other 'starters' who came under their control.

The pressure on the ex-players on the committee has grown with the years, for Boycott's departure at the end of the 1986 campaign severed the last active link with a championship triumph. For the first time in over ninety years the playing staff contained no first-hand experience of success at the highest level. Thus Phil Carrick, in taking over the captaincy, shouldered a heavy and lonely burden.

The winning of the Benson and Hedges Cup in 1987 on balance did more harm than good, creating a dangerous illusion that all was well. BBC commentator Don Mosey reflected the misguided views of many when he claimed in his book *We Don't Play It For Fun* that 'The pattern of Yorkshire cricket history which had been so miserably and unworthily broken during the previous one and a half decades was in that moment somehow restored.' For good measure, he continued: 'God was in his heaven and the sun was shining at Headingley.' The committee shared his misplaced confidence with the result that two years later they were picking up the pieces of the worst season in the county's history and making Martyn Moxon the seventh captain in thirteen years.

In the circumstances, it is easy to believe that anyone charged with writing about ten great post-war Yorkshire cricketers in twenty or thirty years will be stuck with the same list as I have compiled.

There can be no short cuts to bring about a revival and until the whole adminstration is streamlined and the unwieldly committee replaced by a professional management team there is little hope of Yorkshire making a worthwhile impact.

I had very little difficulty in making my choice. Most of them were automatic, although David Bairstow faced strong competition from Jimmy Binks, who was certainly a better wicketkeeper standing up. Binks, quite tall for a wicketkeeper, established a county record of 412 consecutive appearances from his debut in June 1955 to his retirement in 1969 and suffered only one injury — a broken finger which did not interfere with his cricket. The fact that he was able to stand up effectively to the medium pace of Bob Platt, whose natural movement took the ball sharply into the right hander, and Tony Nicholson enabled these bowlers to put additional pressure on the batsmen. Indeed Colin Cowdrey regards one of his most remarkable dismissals in a very long and distinguished career as a leg-side stumping by Binks off Nicholson. One of the handful of Yorkshire cricketers from the East Coast, Hull-born Binks stands very much alongside the best wicketkeepers in the business. Bairstow, though, is unquestionably the best wicketkeeper-batsman to represent the county.

Willie Watson, an elegant and, in the 1953 series with Australia, for example, determined left-hander would have had his supporters, but I finally decided to introduce a note of variety by giving the place that would otherwise have been his to Dickie Bird.

This is because I feel that umpires do not receive sufficient recognition, and it is to Yorkshire's credit that they have produced the best in the world. That is not, incidentally, my opinion only. Cricketers from Melbourne to Manchester, Calcutta to Canterbury and St. John's, Antigua to St. John's Wood, London, agree that Dickie 'makes fewest mistakes', which is the best recommendation of them all. The standards of umpiring in England are incredibly high as the men in the white coats somehow maintain their concentration for six-and-a-half demanding hours — and more — in baking heat and icy blast.

Cricket has been the Yorkshireman's abiding passion for more than 200 years and, with so many clubs flourishing throughout the Broad Acres, the game's future is as safe as anything can be in this dangerous world. On that basis , there is still hope at Headingley.

CHAPTER ONE

Len Hutton

Len Hutton's career is neatly divided into two distinct sections by the Second World War which nearly ended it. When hostilities broke out in September 1939, he was the flowering genius of English cricket with a world record Test score of 364 to his credit, and when peace was restored he became the first professional to captain his country. Between these great achievements came the accident which so seriously threatened his future. Although minor in comparison with the horrific casualties of the time, the damage he sustained to his left arm on March 14, 1941 drew a heavy black cloud across his future.

On the last day of a commando training course with the Army Physical Training Corps Hutton slipped on the mat while attempting a 'fly spring' and, in medical terms, fractured the radius and dislocated the ulna at the base of the left wrist. The outcome was a whole series of operations at the hands of Reginald Broomhead, an orthopaedic surgeon of exceptional patience and skill. Two bone grafts and long periods in hospital over a period of two and a half years left Hutton with his left arm almost two inches shorter than his right. For the right-handed batsmen cricket is, ironically, a left-handed game, with the left side of the body leading the way into any stroke, whether attacking or defensive, and Hutton admitted: 'There were many times when I wondered whether I would ever play cricket again.'

That he returned to become so dominant a force in county and Test cricket is a tribute to both Mr Broomhead's persistence and expertise and his own determination and courage, for he knew only too well that any blow on his arm would almost certainly be fatal so far as his career was concerned.

There is a weight of statistical evidence to guarantee Hutton immortality among cricket lovers throughout the world, but there was far more to the man than mere records. He decorated the game with a stylish grace that earned admiration even in the ranks of the opposition, and the elegant way in which he collected his runs made watching a pleasurable pain for the most enthusiastic supporter of the other side. Hutton remained incapable of an ugly stroke right to the end, for the quality of his play was an extension of his professionalism which added individual colour to the drab basics of technique.

The shy boy who arrived at the Headingley nets as a thirteen-year-old grew into a batsman in the classic style and even after injury he refused to compromise. 'I never really batted without some discomfort after the war,' he said. 'My left wrist would swell painfully, but I was fortunate to be able to play first-class cricket.'

Cricket in Yorkshire has always been instinctively competitive, so the fact that Hutton appeared with Pudsey St Lawrence second eleven at twelve is significant. So, too, is the fact that the opposition's now unknown bowler greeted the arrival of a slender youth with a bat clearly too big for him by lobbing up some gentle donkey drops. These having been despatched to all corners of the field, the bowler reverted to what he fondly believed was fast bowling and met a similar fate.

As a matter of course, Hutton graduated to the senior side when fourteen and was sent in first to partner a former Yorkshire batsman, Edgar Oldroyd, who was not at first exactly pleased to find himself associated with someone twenty-eight years his junior. Increasing familiarity, however,

A youthful Len Hutton goes out to open the Yorkshire innings at Scarborough with Wilf Barber.

bred respect rather than contempt in the mind of the 'old soldier', who set himself to nurture the seeds of greatness.

'We probably made an odd-looking pair,' Hutton conceded. 'He was nicknamed ''Little Ark'' and possessed the most complete defence, having the correct stroke for every ball, no matter how difficult. I could not help but learn standing at the other end each Saturday and I quickly came to appreciate that a sound defence was the foundation of any innings.' Already, of course, Hutton had caught Yorkshire's eye and he duly received an invitation to the nets, making his way through the wintry streets of Leeds to be confronted by

Bill Bowes and Hedley Verity, the most destructive bowling combination in English cricket. The legendary George Hirst, as Yorkshire's coach, studied the youngster's technique as it underwent the most searching examination and, at the end, observed: 'Well done, keep on with that.'

That represented excessive praise, but Hutton never became the victim of conceit. 'No one could ever become big-headed in Yorkshire cricket,' he said. 'You were surrounded by so many great players and there were always the ghosts of the past looking over your shoulder. I did not, in any case, regard myself as being more than above average.' He nevertheless possessed an inner resolve which stood him in good stead as he developed the habit of being dismissed for nought at the beginning of each new phase of his career. The eternally cheerful Maurice Leyland, a magnificent batsman in his own right, called it 'Starting at the bottom.'

Hutton marked his arrival in Minor County cricket with a duck, added another on his debut for Yorkshire and failed to score in his first innings for England against New Zealand. 'That sequence was one of those things that happen,' he reflected. 'I recall when I got my chance with Yorkshire's first team I was run out against Cambridge University at Fenner's probably because I was a bit too eager.'

To put the record straight and balance the picture, Hutton is one of only fifteen players to announce himself to the Australians in Test cricket with a century and, in doing so, he set the pattern which was to stretch into the 1950s as he stood firm, sometimes almost alone, against the 'old enemy'. He played in twenty-seven Tests against Australia, scoring 2,428 runs for an average of 56.46, a figure exceeded only by his famous predecessor Herbert Sutcliffe (66.85) and Surrey's Ken Barrington (63.96).

Australia also endured the agony of fielding out for Hutton's remarkable 364 at the Oval in 1938. Wisden reported that 'No more remarkable exhibition of concentration and endurance has ever been seen on the cricket field,' but Hutton saw things in a different light. 'It was an enormous responsibility to become a national celebrity at twenty-two and I worried quite a lot about fathers bringing their sons to see me. There was always the possibility that I might be out first ball. Anyone can fail, and I realised how much pressure there had been on Don Bradman, who had carried the weight of so much public expectation on his shoulders from his earliest days.'

The same sentiments bothered the naturally thoughtful and introverted Hutton as he approached the previous highest individual score in the series between England and Australia — Bradman's 334 at Headingley in 1930, when Hutton had been an enthralled spectator. 'I was transported to a land of wonderment. I hurried home to Pudsey and somehow persuaded two friends to bowl at me until it became too dark to continue,' Hutton said later and, strangely, that was the last Test cricket he saw until he earned selection in the side to meet New Zealand at Lord's seven years on.

The memory stayed with him and, no doubt, acted as a source of inspiration at the Oval. The contest had advanced well into the third day when Hutton reached 331 and the nation held its collective breath in offices, on street corners and anywhere that provided the opportunity for people to gather together. A population weaned on the instant coverage provided by the portable radio and the television cameras cannot readily appreciate the agony of uncertainty which gripped the country. Would he do it? Had he done it? Hutton himself recalled: 'I could almost feel the tension and Bradman made the most of the situation by crowding me. He stationed himself at silly-on and before each delivery our eyes met. It was a psychological duel which I knew I must win.'

Leslie Fleetwood-Smith, a brilliant if somewhat erratic left-arm spinner, dropped into one of his more economical spells at the crucial moment, pinning Hutton onto the defensive, twice testing the judgement of umpire Frank Chester and the nerves of many millions by appealing for lbw. He was unsuccessful on both occasions. 'The Australian wicketkeeper

Ben Barnett agreed that I got an inside edge on the first and Chester decided that the second was too high and would have cleared the stumps,' recalled Hutton, who relied, as ever in a time of crisis, on a rock-like defence.

'I reasoned that if I could keep control and hold out, Fleetwood-Smith would eventually send down a loose delivery,' he said. 'I had actually been exactly 300 not out after two days and those last runs to beat Bradman seemed to be an awful long time in coming. The period between 300 and 335 felt like the longest part of my innings and I could not prevent myself wondering if they would ever come. Fortunately I was pretty fit then. I had been out of the game with a broken finger and missed the fourth Test, while the break on the Sunday gave me the chance of taking a long rest. Apart from my ambition, I had to take account of the instructions I had received from our captain, Wally Hammond, who wanted a very big score. He wanted me to stay out in the middle for as long as possible. Hammond was so determined to grind the Australians into the ground that when on the Monday, either Maurice Leyland or me lofted a shot, he came down onto the balcony and signalled that we must keep the ball down.' At precisely 12.45 on August 23 the long hop duly arrived and Hutton cut it fiercely to the boundary. The world, or at least that part of it aware of the stroke, went pardonably wild. Hutton's natural delight at his contribution to eventual victory — he finally lofted a ball to cover off the persistent Tiger O'Reilly after batting for 13 hours and 20 minutes — was tinged with a genuine regret that such an awe-inspiring triumph changed the course of a life which was no longer entirely his own, and there is little doubt that he found the intrusion of complete strangers a nuisance.

In any case, Hutton always preferred consistency to brilliance and there is little doubt that, however satisfying that remarkable innings might have been, he took more pleasure from the long sequence of impressive scores which stretched across the summers of 1937, 1938 and 1939. If his first tour — to South Africa in the winter of '38-39 — is taken into account,

Test matches drew huge crowds in the 1948 summer and Len Hutton (left) and Cyril Washbrook, of Lancashire, his regular opening partner for England, had to make their way out to the middle through a mass of well-wishers.

he had an average of slightly better than 61 in the course of a golden period. He celebrated his 23rd birthday on June 23, 1939 with the world more or less at his feet, yet the sombre threat of war clouded his horizons and finally brought an abrupt end to the season.

He scored 238 for once out in the Oval Test against the West Indies and travelled south with his Yorkshire team-mates. He stroked his way to 100 against Kent at Dover, added 103 off the Sussex attack at Brighton and saw the splendid Hedley Verity perform the last of his many magnificent bowling feats as the home side were dismissed for 33.

Hutton finished the campaign a mere 27 runs short of 3,000, and there can surely be no doubt that he would have amassed many more runs during the next six years but for the sickening conflict which brought the death in action of Verity, a player Hutton so much admired. He lost unquestionably the best years of his cricketing life and sustained the injury which forced him almost to begin again, so he cannot have approached the revival of first-class cricket and the Victory Tests of 1945 with total confidence.

He opened the England innings with Flight Sergeant Cyril Washbrook, who subsequently became his regular partner in one of England's more enduring first-wicket associations, and he quietly settled back into the groove with innings of 104 and 69 in the third game against a very strong opposition. He worked relentlessly at his game, practising with an almost religious fervour as he returned to his roots at Pudsey St Lawrence on Saturdays to make sure that he got some serious cricket. Missing no opportunity to adjust to his slightly remodelled technique, he gradually refound his surest touch and he was ready when, in 1946, county cricket resumed on a proper basis.

The post-war period contained many highlights as Hutton emphasised just how much had been lost to the war. At Sydney on the 1946-47 tour, when England were hardly ready for Test cricket, he played one of the great short innings of all time, making only 37 but playing with such sublime authority that all who saw it were overwhelmed by its sheer brilliance. Those runs came in twenty glorious minutes, but Hutton remained slightly bemused by the people who rated the innings above his 364, and it is a strange thing that in later years his rate of progress during that famous Oval occasion attracted some criticism.

Hutton understood the importance of taking full advantage of winning the toss and shaped his innings to meet the circumstances — as he was to do so often between 1946 and his retirement in 1955. For all the solid ability of Washbrook and the dashing skills of the Middlesex 'twins', Bill Edrich and Denis Compton, Hutton provided the spinal cord of the England innings during a period when the Australians held a clear advantage in the batting of Bradman and the bowling of Ray Lindwall and Keith Miller. They were the outstanding figures in a truly great team against whom England struggled in vain.

Hutton scored readily in 1946, '47 and '48 before reaching new peaks in '49. Only three batsmen have ever made 3,500 runs in a season — Edrich, Compton and Tom Hayward, of Surrey — but Hutton reached 3,429 in that year for an average of 68.58. He did not quite manage 1,000 by the end of May, a feat which has attracted much attention down the years, but he became only the fourth batsman to score 1,000 in two months of the same summer — 1,294 in June and 1,050 in August. The figure for June remains the highest in any month and, with the steady reduction in the first-class programme, that aggregate is never likely to be challenged in the future.

Incredibly, in the middle of June, Hutton was dismissed for nought in three successive innings. One of these came against New Zealand and the other two represented a 'pair' against Worcestershire. The Test match duck, however, followed a stylish 101 at Headingley and he compiled twelve centuries in all. 'By the end of that summer I was utterly exhausted,' he said. 'I found myself on the field for at least part of nearly every day and I suppose I came close to another record in terms of the miles covered by a player.

'The boundaries have been brought in and regularised in recent times, but some of the grounds could be very testing. The Oval was a vast expanse and all-run fives were by no means rare, particularly from the Vauxhall End. I remember all too clearly some long, hot and tiring days there.'

Weary or not, Hutton still had the strength and the enthusiasm to provide his almost inevitable Scarborough Festival century as the curtain came down on the campaign, and it can be safely said that in 1949 Hutton reached full maturity as a batsman. He displayed to perfection every stroke in the book, and, while the cover drive remained the hallmark of his artistry, he scored handsomely in every area. The year left him with nothing else to prove as a batsman, but he had yet another great service to render his country — as the first professional captain.

As events in that direction moved towards an historic conclusion, Hutton completed his 100th century on the 16th of July, 1951, satisfyingly against Surrey at the Oval, where the greatest England opener, Jack Hobbs, to whom he was often compared, had collected so many of his runs. He also featured in an unusual incident in the final Test match against South Africa on the same ground, becoming the only batsman in Test history to be given out 'obstructing the field.' Athol Rowan was bowling and Hutton recalled: 'I tried to sweep to leg, but the ball struck me on the left glove and ran up my arm. Next thing I saw it in front of my eyes. I thought the ball might drop onto my wicket, so I attempted to brush it away with the back of my bat.' Meanwhile, South African wicketkeeper Russell Endean had moved forward in the hope of completing a catch, although Hutton insisted: 'I was not trying to put him off.' On appeal umpires Dai Davies and Frank Chester, as the sole judges of fact, ruled him out, although the laws state: 'The striker may guard his wicket with his bat or any other part of his person other than his hands.' Without doubt, on that occasion the umpires applied another law which states: 'The striker, on appeal, shall be out should wilful destruction by either batsmen prevent a catch being made. This shall apply even though the striker causes obstruction in lawfully guarding his wicket.'

There was no argument about Hutton's place at the forefront of English cricket in 1952. He had earned a position as an elder statesman among the players and his qualifications as captain were impressive. In these egalitarian days, it is difficult to understand the arguments against his appointment, although, at the time, these were passionate enough.

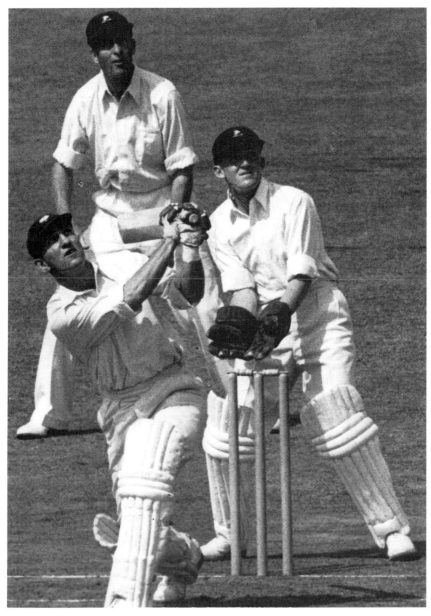

More runs for Len Hutton as he despatches the ball high over mid-wicket in
the approved manner.

Lord Hawke, the father figure of Yorkshire cricket, had
expressed the strongly held views of many some thirty years
previously when he said: 'Please God, no professional shall
ever captain England.' Hobbs had actually deputised when

Arthur Carr was taken ill against Australia at Manchester in 1926 and attempts by the more sensitive historians have been made to persuade the modern world that Hawke merely meant that he hoped there would always be an amateur good enough to do the job, but such a convenient explanation misses the social point. Even in the 1950s there was an order in all things, and the wealthy aristocrats who ruled cricket regarded the professionals largely as tradesmen, admirable in their own way but not fitted to lead.

Hutton had grown up to appreciate that there was a clear dividing line between professionals and amateurs. Indeed, he played at Lord's on several occasions before he actually entered the holy of holies, the pavilion. 'The professionals' changing rooms were situated near to where the Warner Stand is now, with the old Press box immediately above it, and the professionals went onto the field through their own gate. We did not resent this because we understood the traditions which existed at Lord's.'

The traditionalists did not surrender without a fight and they manned the barricades with a good deal of fervour. They put forward David Sheppard, of Cambridge University and Sussex, which may well have caused him a good deal of embarrassment. Certainly, like Hutton, he kept his own counsel and both men behaved with a calm dignity which took at least some heat out of the situation.

Hutton himself had a deep regard for many of the amateur captains with whom he had come into contact. 'They encouraged a fine spirit of comradeship in cricket,' he said. 'In Yorkshire the amateur captain led the team and allowed the professionals to get on with the job. They maintained discipline, put the interests of the game first and got the best out of the team, so it did not matter too much that they were not good enough as players.'

There could never have been any serious comparisons between the 35-year-old Hutton, with his wealth of experience and a proven track record, and the 23-year-old Sheppard, with four Test matches to his credit. Any resistance to Hutton had to be based on the amateur tradition, which has much to commend it even today when all other things are equal, but they were clearly not equal in 1952. Commonsense prevailed and the selectors — Norman Yardley, Bob Wyatt, Freddie Brown and Les Ames — pursued the logical course and went for Hutton. Being appointed to such high office was one thing, succeeding represented another challenge altogether, particularly as Hutton knew only too well that all eyes were on both his performance and his behaviour.

The slightest slip would have provided the amateur lobby with eagerly awaited ammunition. He did not have much trouble in leading his side to a three-nil victory over the Indians, who found the pace and hostility of the emerging Fred Trueman altogether too much, but Australia offered a much sterner test in the following year. 'I would not have been human if I had not had some misgivings when I became captain,' said Hutton. 'Obviously my appointment did not meet with universal approval and I wondered how Lord's, the citadel of tradition, would react to me. There were some difficulties but I found to my relief that every M.C.C. official gave me his complete support. Additionally, the majority of the rank and file M.C.C. members were favourably disposed towards me. When I became captain, our cricket had taken three severe hammerings from the Australians. In 1946 and 1950 Australians regarded our touring sides as a bunch of mugs and it is no fun being looked on in that way. I got fed up being told how to play by Australians.

'I was determined to put England cricket back on top. I wanted to give a lead to our young cricketers. You cannot raise cricketers on failure and that has been true for every generation.

'I knew that some other players might not like my way because I had a different attitude. I could never bring myself to joke with a bowler I intended to hit for four next ball. The one thing from which I could eventually take comfort was the fact that my methods succeeded.'

Hutton duly went on to regain the Ashes, the decisive victory arriving in the last Test at the Oval after England's hopes had been kept alive by two stern rearguard actions at Lord's and Headingley. Without being quite at his imperious best, Hutton contributed a superb 145 at Lord's and the highest score of the match at the Oval as England completed their first home victory over the Australians since 1926.

Looking back, Hutton recalled: 'It took quite a while for the fact that we had won to sink in, for there had been so many dramas and changes of fortune during the series. There had been times of crisis, notably when Willie Watson and Trevor Bailey resisted so gallantly at Lord's. I lost the toss in all five games and I desperately wanted to bat first at the Oval, for I believed there would be some assistance for the spinners in the later stages, which proved to be the case.' England had to make 132 in the fourth innings and they got home by the comfortable-looking margin of eight wickets.

It might be imagined that Hutton, having achieved so much and lifted England to a position of eminence among the cricketing nations, would be safe from the criticism of lesser mortals at least for a decent period of time. Unfortunately, the tour to the West Indies in 1953-54 turned out to be a far from pleasant business. The result was satisfactory enough as England shared the series 2-2 after being two down and Hutton played considerably more than his part in averaging 150 for the last three games, but he was weighed down by all manner of difficulties.

He scored 169 at Georgetown and 205 at Kingston, where he occupied the crease for some nine hours, and after that epic innings he inadvertently ignored the congratulations of Jamaica's chief minister Mr Alex Bustamante. As soon as he realised there might have been a misunderstanding, Hutton moved quickly to put things right and Mr Bustamante, for his part, was gracious, but those who supported the view that a professional had been elevated above his station found scope for mischief.

Hutton's party also had a lot of trouble with the umpiring, some of the senior players were a bit short on loyalty, the choice of Charles Palmer as manager was a mistake and, under pressure, the captain, who had never been 'hail fellow, well met,' lacked perhaps the real authority to exert himself. In his own assessment: 'The trip left me physically and mentally drained and I feel that the experience probably took two years off my career.

'There was a lot of tension and stress in that tour and these are the elements which are missing from cricket at lower level. We had cricketers on that trip who could play the strokes, but the question I found myself continually asking concerned whether they could play them under the tensions that existed.'

Hutton subsequently defended Palmer, saying: 'No manager could have tried harder, been more diplomatic or done his onerous job better', but having a manager who also played in the team, making his solitary Test appearance, hardly made a lot of sense. The lines of demarcation became too thinly drawn. England lost the first two Tests in which they batted badly and, as the series had been unofficially regarded as being for the world championship, the tension grew.

They recovered in the third match at Georgetown, where the infamous riot broke out. It followed a straightforward run-out decision against Cliff McWatt which ended the eighth-wicket partnership on 99. A hail of missiles rained on the ground and the umpires looked to the safety of the pavilion, but England, in a winning position with West Indies on 238 for eight in reply to 435, stood firm. 'It never occurred to me or the team to leave the field,' said Hutton, whose main concern lay in pressing home his obvious advantage. It all came right in the end. A cable of congratulations for a 'fine example in difficult conditions' arrived from Lord's and England won.

Taking everything into account, Hutton emerged with his reputation even higher as another success followed at Kingston, but the cricket politicians, ignoring all that did not fit in with their preconceived theories, revived the captaincy debate, encouraged by the fact that Hutton managed to play in only the first and last Tests of 1954 against Pakistan due to illness. Sheppard deputised, but could hardly be regarded as a serious rival as he had already made it clear that his future lay within the ministry of the Church of England. Even so, it began to be whispered in influential circles that 'Sheppard is the man to take England to Australia', the advocates of this idea usually adding that Hutton would be able to concentrate on his batting.

Although already appointed for Australia, Hutton's cause was not helped when, as he returned to captain England at the Oval, the scene of his great Ashes triumph, Pakistan, who shared their first rubber in this country 1-1, gained a famous victory. He had a lean time with the bat, too, managing only 0, 14 and 5. He said: 'The season was virtually written off for me.' The medical men did not pass him fit to tour Australia until mid-summer, but once more he received the inevitable vote and Sheppard did not go to Australia in any capacity.

The tour to Australia began disastrously at Brisbane, where Hutton put in Australia and England lost by an innings. 'I misread the pitch and that was simply all there was to it,' Hutton recalled. 'I had hoped to put Australia on the defensive, but we dropped a whole series of catches in the worst display of fielding I endured as captain.'

Things took a turn for the better when Frank Tyson found his most destructive rhythm and carried England to a 3-1 success which earned the Northamptonshire pace bowler the nickname of 'Typhoon' and Hutton an even more distinguished place in history. Tyson did not make an immediate impact and the policy of preferring him to Trueman as a 'shot in the dark' looked foolish until, under the guidance of Hutton and Bowes, by then a journalist covering the tour, he shortened his run and became much more effective.

On Hutton's return from Australia, M.C.C. altered their rules to make him an honorary life member while he was still playing, but he was denied the pleasure of leading England against South Africa in the following summer by back trouble which brought his retirement. Suffering from arthritis of the spine, Hutton kept going on pain-killing tablets in Australia, and his last century for Yorkshire amounted to 194 off the Nottinghamshire attack on Trent Bridge. 'I realised that there was something seriously wrong and, although I would have liked to play for two or three more seasons, enjoying my cricket, I accepted that I could not continue,' he admitted.

The demanding life as a first-class cricketer put a great strain on Hutton's far from robust physique. 'My frame should probably have been bigger for the job,' he felt. 'I have often thought that my generation played too much first-class cricket. As a consequence our appetites were occasionally dulled. I played in 814 matches and scored 40,140 runs, while, in comparison, Bradman made only 338 appearances for 28,067. I do not suggest for a minute that he would not have made an enormous impact on English cricket had he joined a county side, for he had a superb technique, but I do feel that he was spared the rigours of the English circuit and benefited.

'In the 1970s and '80s gaps appeared in the programme and various one-day competitions were introduced to provide a variety denied to us. I would have liked to play some limited-overs cricket because, although this form of the game is often blamed for the decline in standards, I believe that cricketers should be able to adapt.

'I do not think that the Sunday League has been good for cricket, because there has to be something wrong when restricting the scoring is more important than taking wickets, and really at least fifty overs for each side are necessary to create circumstances for a proper match.'

In some minds Hutton has remained a cautious, over-defensive figure, but his own assessment of his approach as captain is that of a realist. 'I defended when necessary and attacked whenever I had the chance,' he said. 'Cricket is a game you cannot plan in advance. Situations change within half an hour, a short time in relation to the thirty hours of a

Test match or, even, the nineteen of a county championship fixture. If you receive a half-volley as a batsman you hit it for four, no matter what the circumstances. Every player of international class has always known that.'

His main preoccupation lay with winning the match and a quick, dashing 30 or 40 rarely achieves that aim. His often flawless defence made him a match-winner on difficult pitches when the ball reared or spun viciously and his wide range of forcing strokes enabled him to give the bowlers time in which to do their job. Hutton was, in fact, the complete batsman who studied the game carefully to overcome difficulties and make the most of his enormous talent.

CAREER DETAILS

FOR ENGLAND (1937-55)

Hutton appeared in 79 Tests and captained England on 23 occasions. He scored 6,971 runs for an average of 56.67, hitting 19 centuries with a highest score of 364 against Australia at the Oval in 1938. He took three wickets at an average of 77.33 and held 57 catches.

FOR YORKSHIRE (1934-55)

Hutton completed 465 innings and scored 24,807 runs for an average of 53.34. He hit 85 centuries with a highest score of 280 not out against Hampshire in 1939. He completed 1,000 runs in a season 12 times, his best being 2,640 in 1949. He took 154 wickets for an average of 27.40.

IN FIRST-CLASS CRICKET (1934-60)

Hutton completed 723 innings and scored 40,140 runs for an average of 55.51. He hit 129 centuries. He completed 1,000 runs in a season 17 times, his best being 3,429 in 1949. Hutton claimed 173 wickets at 29.42 runs each.

Sir Leonard was elected president of Yorkshire at the annual meeting in Sheffield on February 24, 1990.

CHAPTER TWO

Johnny Wardle

Johnny Wardle earned an unchallenged reputation as the 'Clown Prince' of Yorkshire cricket, the jester who could create laughter among the spectators without, for one second, sacrificing anything in terms of application out in the middle. His career as a left-arm spinner, however, was never really a happy one and there was always the potential for tears behind the smiles.

He could convulse the crowd by pausing on his way back to the pavilion, having had his stumps shattered by the opposition attack, to enquire with an air of studious interest: 'Did it look out from here?' He was also regarded by his colleagues as being moody and introverted and he admitted that he rarely felt secure as a cricketer. His inner doubts were the consequence of many disappointments, from the earliest days when he failed to receive his cap at Wath-on-Dearne Grammar School, even though he had so clearly earned one with his all-round skills. 'I was halfway out of my seat at the presentation ceremony when it dawned on me that they were calling out another boy,' he recalled. 'I just could not accept the unfairness of it all and I felt the hurt for a long time.'

His formative years with Yorkshire were blighted by the massive burden of sheer hard work forced on him by circumstances and eventually he rebelled, to be sacked in the most spectacular row to rock the county in the pre-Boycott era.

Wardle also remained bitter about the fact that his opportunities with England were so severely restricted by Tony Lock, his great rival from Surrey, who ran into trouble because of a suspect action and was regarded by many as a 'chucker'. The final tragedy brought Wardle's early death in 1985 at the age of sixty-two, shortly after he had agreed to become Yorkshire's specialist bowling coach.

Bob Appleyard, Wardle's great slow bowling partner with the county in the 1950s, believes: 'Yorkshire lost the most experienced member of their team when they got rid of Johnny in 1958 and the club lost the best bowling coach in the world when he died. I have played with and against many great cricketers, but I have never met anyone who knew as much about bowling. He could talk for hours about cricket and he never missed anything.' Ray Illingworth, one of the shrewdest judges in the game, agrees with that assessment, saying: 'Johnny was the complete professional. He put cricket right at the top of his priorities and he gave a great deal of thought to everything he did.'

On the other side of the coin, Wardle had a sharp tongue, and many a youngster trying to make his way in the Yorkshire side took the full brunt of his sarcasm. Mike Cowan, a more than useful left-arm seamer, experienced some nightmare moments in the field when he failed to take a number of catches off Wardle's bowling and lived in fear of making another mistake. Illingworth also crossed swords with him. 'I soon got fed up with his attitude,' he said. 'I dropped a catch off him and he tore into me, so I decided that I had to stand up for myself. I told him in no uncertain terms that we were all trying very hard and that no one deliberately missed chances. I also pointed out that he was making things a lot worse by putting extra pressure on the younger players in the side. After that we got on very well.'

Wardle became two bowlers in one for the county, for he had a unique talent in being able to bowl both orthodox left-arm spin and the back-of-the-hand stuff — the ball that turned

Johnny Wardle, a keen student of the game and a determined competitor.

from leg to off, the chinaman, turning into the bat, and the googly, which looked as though it should be an offbreak to the right-hander but which actually turned sharply the other way. In the opinion of many widely experienced players and administrators no other left-arm spinner in the history of first-class cricket mastered such variety by adding the essential degree of accuracy.

As is the case with most truly great bowlers, Wardle broadened his skills by thoughtful experiment, beginning at an early age.

A naturally talented and powerfully built athlete, he showed promise as a Rugby Union full-back and rather more as a left-winger at soccer, attracting the attention of Wolverhampton Wanderers, for whom he had trials. 'I suppose I was pretty strong on the ball and packed a useful shot, but I felt I lacked the pace to make the grade. Injury finally persuaded me to put cricket first and I am certain that I made the right decision,' he said.

Like most slow bowlers, Wardle fancied his chances as a seamer initially. 'I used to race in and really let go as a lad,' he admitted, 'but I worked out that I was not tall enough or quick enough to be really successful, so I looked for the means to beat the batsmen in other directions. I tried giving the ball a flip in various ways and eventually produced the chinaman while still operating at around medium-pace.'

Forcing his way into the Yorkshire side immediately after the war was not a straightforward business. The leagues bristled with competition, and when Arthur Booth retired after briefly filling the gap left by the death in action of Hedley Verity, Wardle had to contend with the challenge from Alan Mason. In winning the vote and gaining his cap, Wardle made the most of some favourable conditions, but, instead of slipping into the role of attacking left-arm spinner, he found himself compensating for the departure of stalwarts such as Bill Bowes and Frank Smailes. Yorkshire's attack was desperately thin, so Wardle even took the new ball and reverted to his old seam up style before switching as the shine disappeared. His work-rate was remarkable.

He bowled 1,638 overs in 1950, 1,375 in 1951, 1,847.2 in 1952 and 1,606.2 in 1953, and it is not stretching the point to suggest that had he not been available, Yorkshire might well have collapsed. This long and arduous run followed a period in which the county tried to change Wardle's action. They dropped him in 1949 and suggested that he should aim to emulate the classic cartwheel pose of Wilfred Rhodes. To his credit, Wardle tried, but failed. Comparison with Rhodes and Verity was an albatross which hung around Wardle's neck and both the Press and the public often resented his attempts to improvise. 'I knew all along that if I tried the back of the hand stuff and it went wrong I would get it in the neck,' he said.

Wardle certainly made his mark by carrying the Yorkshire attack until Brian Close, Appleyard and Fred Trueman arrived on the scene, but the feeling persisted that the county had not really had the best out of him. How much more successful might he not have been had his extraordinary talent been given full reign. His great triumph on the tour to South Africa in 1956-57 underlined the largely unexplored possibilities.

His 90 wickets cost 12.25 runs each and he gained a high proportion of them with wrist spin. His return in the Test series amounted to twenty-six wickets at 13.80, and against Orange Free State at Bloemfontein he bewildered and ensnared fourteen victims in a single day on a pretty good batting strip. Even then, when Wardle had every South African batsman in a state of acute anxiety, Peter May, his captain, adopted a negative approach. 'He asked me not to bowl the chinaman, particularly against Trevor Goddard, the South African opener, at Capetown,' Wardle claimed. 'I reckoned it was no good sticking to the orthodox and letting him play himself in because I had been put on from the start of the South African innings as a match-winner. I talked May round and did Goddard fairly easily.' Wardle finished with twelve for 89 and Wally Hammond, the former England captain, and one of the greatest of all-rounders, insisted that he did not accept that anyone could ever have bowled wrist spin with such incredible accuracy.

Wardle might have been thought to be at the height of his powers, but he still experienced serious doubt about his place in the scheme of things. Lock also had a place in the South African party and Wardle confided at the time: 'I feel that if I do not keep on doing well, I shall be out.' He had given impetus to his Test career in the best possible way by gaining an lbw decision against West Indies opener Jeff Stolmyer with his first ball in this country. 'A bit of a loosener, but I dropped it right on length and line,' he said. Things did not go all that smoothly, though, and there is little doubt that Wardle became bitter about his treatment at the hands of the selectors.

The most crippling blow to his pride came at Manchester in 1953 as England moved towards ending a long period of Australian dominance by regaining the Ashes. The tourists had held the initiative for much of a rain-affected game, with England on the defensive until a fantastic last hour, in the course of which Wardle took four wickets for seven runs in five overs. Australia were reduced to 35 for eight and, although a draw had been inevitable throughout their second innings, they displayed such uncertainty against the spinning ball that Wardle established a massive psychological advantage.

Indeed, to try and hide their embarrassment, the Australians went to some lengths to point out that they had not been worried. 'We just got a bit careless because there was nothing at stake,' their official line suggested. All the same, no Test batsman readily throws away his wicket, whatever the situation, and most English followers were inclined to think that they were whistling furiously in the dark. The England selectors, however, dropped Wardle and recalled Lock for Leeds and the Oval, where matters came to a successful conclusion. Victory by 1-0 in the Ashes series went a long way towards justifying the selectors, but Wardle would not have been human if he had not nursed a grievance. Few men have lost their place at any level after taking four for seven.

'I simply could not see the justice,' explained Wardle, whose bitterness developed into a personal dislike to Lock. Whenever Yorkshire and Surrey were in opposition, Wardle was likely to gaze out onto the field when his side were batting and exclaim: 'Just look at the bastard throwing out there.' Lock pushed the ball through much quicker than Wardle and added a faster ball for good measure, so that some people thought he threw just about everything. Umpires took a much more tolerant view of this irregularity in the 1950s, when officialdom turned a blind eye and let people get on with the game. Nevertheless, Lock had to remodel his style completely in 1959, when the facts caught up with him, a turn of events which provided little consolation to Wardle, who had sat and suffered for so long.

'People used to argue that it did not matter about a slow bowler throwing because he was not going to hurt anyone,' Wardle said. 'To my mind that is nonsense. The laws are there to be obeyed and a bowler who throws the ball gets an unfair advantage over the others. He takes wickets to which he is not entitled.

'I used to spend two or three hours working to get a wicket, trying to outwit the batsman, which is why it annoyed me to see a catch go down. That one false stroke probably resulted from a carefully laid trap and once it had failed to bring the wicket it could mean that, at best, I had to start all over again. Lock fired the ball in and seemed to want a wicket with every ball. That could never have been my way, although I know many people regarded me as an aggressive cricketer.

'It was suggested, too, that we could have been used in partnership. At one stage Yorkshire considered playing two slow left-arm bowlers and that would have given me more opportunity to use the chinaman. Lock and I were very different in every way.' It was not to be, however, and at international level Wardle's ambitions were only partially fulfilled.

Lock was not entirely to blame for the fact that Wardle played his last match for his country on that 1956-57 tour to South Africa. The Surrey man appeared in all five Tests when New Zealand toured in 1958, but Wardle gained selection for the M.C.C. party to visit Australia in the winter of 1958-59. But four days after his inclusion among the seventeen came the shock announcement that Yorkshire were to 'dispense with his services.' That news broke over the busy heads of the Press at the close of play in the Somerset match at Sheffield, where secretary John Nash issued a brief statement. It read: 'The Yorkshire Committee have informed J.H. Wardle that they will not be calling on his services at the end of the season.' Asked to reconcile that with Wardle's selection for the tour, Brian Sellers, who was both a selector and a member of the Yorkshire committee, commented: 'They are two different things. He may be good enough for England but not good enough for Yorkshire.'

Inevitably, the Yorkshire public reacted strongly to the sacking of one of their favourite figures, while Wardle burst into print to explain his side of the argument. He launched a vicious attack on the county captain Ronnie Burnet, who was in his first season, and said: 'Yorkshire sacked me because I refused to accept the authority of a quite hopeless old man appointed captain. He knew nothing about first-class cricket and was quite incompetent.'

Burnet undoubtedly arrived on the scene lacking genuine credentials. He came into office direct from the Bradford League and the county second team, having proved himself to be a useful club cricketer and a strong-minded leader. Wardle felt that he might have been given the job himself, for, with Willie Watson having moved on to Leicestershire, he had seniority on his side. The county committee, however, had other ideas and, worried by what they regarded as a decline in the standards of behaviour, they went outside the club's senior ranks.

Wardle was not, it transpired, their second or third choice. Had Burnet not been available, they were prepared to turn to another Bradford League amateur, Derek Blackburn, while they wanted to make Vic Wilson senior professional. Burnet supported Wardle for this latter role. 'I argued with the committee that he had to be given his chance and that if he did his job correctly there would be no problems. I wanted to put everything on a firm and fair footing.' Wardle did, in fact, captain Yorkshire when Burnet stood down through injury, but this period represented no more than a calm before the storm.

There has always been something of a mystery about the events which led to Wardle's demise. Sellers, speaking at the time when Yorkshire revealed their intention to release him at the end of the 1958 season, said: 'There was no indication of all this happening four days ago when I helped to pick the England touring party for Australia. It was a lightning decision and not discussed until this afternoon. Yorkshire are looking to give chances to a number of very promising young players and are in the process of making room for them.' As the county had also let two other Test cricketers in Appleyard and Frank Lowson go, his observation carried a lot of conviction.

After Wardle had made his views public, though, and thus caused the M.C.C. to withdraw his invitation to tour, Yorkshire issued another statement. This one read: 'The Yorkshire County Cricket Club committee regret the unpleasant publicity given to their decision to dispense with the services of J.H. Wardle after the present season. In the past years Wardle has been warned on several occasions that his general behaviour on the field and in the dressing room left much to be desired. As no improvement was shown this year the decision to dispense with his services was made. It was unanimously considered that it was essential to have discipline and a happy and loyal team before a lasting improvement could be expected.

'It is felt that the recent articles published in the *Daily Mail* fully justify the committee's decision. Wardle broke his contract when he wrote those articles without first obtaining permission from the committee and, therefore, they terminated his contract forthwith.'

This statement clearly contradicted Sellers, who ruled Yorkshire cricket with a rod of iron, and Wardle denied receiving any official warnings. 'The decision to get rid of me came as a complete surprise,' he said. 'I felt I had fifteen good years of county cricket left in me and I simply could not understand why I had been thrown on one side. The criticism upset me and I probably acted hastily in putting my name to newspaper articles written in the heat of the moment. What did really gall me was that on the quiet the committee, or at least some of those on it, had asked me to keep an eye on Burnet, to give him advice when he needed it. I did my best, but sometimes he did not seem to take too much notice. I also expressed my views that some of the younger players did not put enough effort into their cricket. I had all my chats with Burnet in private and thought we were putting the team on the right path. Most people did not know all the ins and outs of what happened and I am not sure that I appreciated all that took place myself.'

Burnet, for his part, regretted Wardle's attitude. He recalls that his most experienced player did not do a lot for team spirit and resented any suggestions from the captain. Accusations of 'not trying' or at least 'not trying hard enough all the time' were bandied about and when Burnet attended a committee meeting at Sheffield he recommended that Wardle be removed from the side. The subject of the meeting, meanwhile, was acting as captain and taking six wickets for 46 runs. Burnet went on to win the championship with a young untried team in the following season and commented: 'I was truly sorry that Wardle did not share in that triumph. I had the greatest respect for him as a player, but I remain convinced that he had become sour and disillusioned. We could not afford his attitude.'

Had Wardle quietly accepted things at Yorkshire, he would have toured Australia. The captain Peter May said: 'I needed Wardle and wanted him. I was very sorry when he had to be withdrawn from my party.' He would also have extended his life on the county circuit, for Nottinghamshire forwarded a request for permission to make him a special registration for 1959 and put forward a very generous offer. Instead, he drifted into Lancashire League cricket with Nelson and Rishton and also featured in the Minor Counties' competition with Cambridgeshire. 'I had some happy times,' he recalled, 'but it was not the same as playing for Yorkshire and England by a long chalk. It was my own fault, though, so I had to make the best of it.' Possibly the most pertinent comment came in the homely, straightforward atmosphere of a miners' club in South Elmsall. Wardle, as guest speaker, was asked bluntly: 'Johnny, doesn't tha think tha's bin a bloody fooil?' Wardle did not hesitate in his reply. 'Aye, I reckon I have,' he acknowledged.

Wardle made the first gesture of reconciliation when he met Burnet at Scarborough in 1959 and offered his congratulations on the championship victory, but almost twenty years were to elapse before he returned to the fold. He was elected an honorary life member in 1977, by which time he had rescued offspinner Geoff Cope's career. Cope had been banned in 1972 for throwing and sent to see Wardle. 'I stood in awe of him, because he had been one of my heroes as a boy,' says Cope, 'but he soon put me at my ease. He said from the first day that if I did exactly as he told me I would play for England, an opinion which took some believing at the time. My spirits were low and I could not believe him. He took my action apart and I bowled from nine o'clock in the morning until early evening. He watched and encouraged. There were times when I could only hit the roof of the net and the sides with my deliveries, but he made me persevere.

'Eventually everything clicked and I not only returned to play with Yorkshire, but I did exactly what he had told me I would and represented England. His knowledge of the game was incredible. Phil Carrick, my left-arm spin partner in the Yorkshire team, had some trouble running down the line of the stumps. He discussed this with me because he was quite worried and I agreed to contact Johnny and seek his advice. I duly rang up and mentioned Phil's name. Before I could say anything else, Johnny chipped in. "I know exactly what you are going to ask me about. He wants to cure his fault of running onto the wicket." He had not only seen the problem, but he had an instant cure.'

Shortly before his death, Wardle accepted an invitation to become Yorkshire's assistant bowling coach. The title underplayed the extent of his influence, for no one in the country was better equipped to offer guidance. He would have been assistant to no one had he been able to take up his duties as planned on March 1, 1985. Unfortunately, he fell ill and never really recovered. Talking about his role, though, he said. 'One of Yorkshire's faults is that some of the older players live in the past and give the impression that things are no longer so good as they were. Some young players cannot stand talking to them. They are immediately put on the defensive and made to feel inferior. That is not the way to bring out the best in boys. The game is as good as it ever was, although it is played in different conditions.

'Cricket is about watching and learning. I cannot accept the practice of players sitting in the dressing room and not keeping a close eye on events on the field. I am convinced that it is vital to watch every ball. You pick up so many things by observation and study. Willie Watson could pick out my googly from square leg before I had delivered. I cocked my wrist differently and he noticed. I want to get Yorkshire's bowlers thinking about what they are trying to do.

'Above all, cricket is a game that should be enjoyed. There are so many different facets about playing and about the preparations. There is so much that can be done by flight and change of pace by a slow bowler. You can let the ball go at more or less the same speed for six deliveries and yet make each of them slightly different. You can let it go early or late to create problems for the batsmen even if there is no great assistance in the pitch and the ball is not turning much.'

In the previous summer, Wardle had been cajoled into his first cricket match for twelve years. He could not resist the temptation to indulge his fancy for the chinaman and the googly and took seven wickets for 50 runs in nineteen overs. 'One batsman was stumped when he missed the googly and dislocated his shoulder trying to get back into his crease,' he recalled.

Wardle's natural ability at ball games enabled him to get down to two handicap at golf and he competed with same fierce determination whether the stakes were twenty pence or twenty pounds.

Statistically Wardle did not make a great mark with the bat, although he by no means lacked skill in that direction. He did not fit into the general pattern of Yorkshire's left-arm bowlers by batting right-handed and he usually adopted a fairly robust approach. He came close enough to the double in 1950 with 733 runs and 174 wickets to persuade some county officials that he could be a genuine all-rounder, but the entertainer in him invariably undermined any resolve to 'play sensibly.' In Wardle's own words: 'I always thought it a good idea to get the runs while I could.' Even in times of apparent crisis he took the fight to the bowlers and it is a remarkable fact that more than 60 per cent of his 5,765 runs for Yorkshire came in boundaries. His tally of 147 sixes must put him somewhere near the head of the county figures in that big-hitting field.

One of his almost forgotten feats with the bat had an enormous influence on the outcome of the 1954-55 Ashes series in Australia, when Len Hutton's side gained their first rubber there in twenty-two years. England, of course, had been thrashed by an innings and 154 in the first Test at Brisbane. Wardle did not play in that game, but earned selection for the second Test at Sydney, where despite a two-hour 30 from the captain on a difficult pitch, England were in desperate trouble on the first day. He top-scored in a modest innings of 154, hitting a bright and breezy 35 to share in a last-wicket stand of 43 with Brian Statham. Those few runs paved the way for a success that turned the tables with a vengeance and set up a famous triumph. The feeling lingered, however, that, so far as Wardle was concerned, batting, although enjoyable in its way, served merely as an adjunct to the serious business of bowling.

Norman Yardley, who led the Yorkshire side during Wardle's formative years, summed him up: 'He was a great cricketer and when he cultivated his chinaman he doubled his value to the team. He followed worthily in the great tradition of Yorkshire left-arm spinners. Although in his orthodox role he was probably slightly below the highest class, the combination of the two styles made him a player to be respected and feared in Test matches. He was also a great thinker. He did nothing on the field without a clear sense of purpose and was one of the greatest favourites with the spectators of all time.'

CAREER DETAILS

FOR ENGLAND (1948-57)

Wardle appeared in 28 Tests. He scored 653 runs for an average of 19.78, with a highest score of 66 against West Indies in 1953-54. He claimed 102 wickets for an average of 20.39, his best return being seven for 36 against South Africa at Cape Town, 1957.

FOR YORKSHIRE (1946-58)

Wardle completed 361 innings for Yorkshire, scoring 5,756 runs for an average of 15.96. He had a highest score of 79 against Lancashire at Old Trafford in 1951. He took 1,539 wickets for an average of 181.13. Wardle claimed 100 wickets in a season on ten occasions, his best being 172 in 1950.

IN FIRST-CLASS CRICKET (1946-67)

Wardle completed 456 innings and scored 7,333 runs for an average of 16.08. He claimed 1,846 wickets for an average of 18.97. His outstanding bowling performances were 9 for 25 against Lancashire at Old Trafford in 1954 and 9 for 48 against Sussex at Hull in the same season.

CHAPTER THREE

Brian Close

The world was a bright place full of promise for Brian Close in 1949. The powerfully built youngster who batted left-handed and bowled right hand made a remarkable impact on Yorkshire and England cricket in his first full season, achieving a spectcular hat-trick. He became the youngest player to do the double — 1,000 runs and 100 wickets — the youngest to appear for England at the tender age of eighteen years and 149 days, and the youngest to be awarded a county cap. His life represented the heady stuff of which schoolboys' dreams are made and it appeared inevitable that he would go on to break records and dominate the scene for years. In reality, however, he never quite came to terms with his potential and actually earned only irregular selection for his country.

Close himself believes that his unhappy experiences on the 1950-51 tour to Australia under the captaincy of Freddie Brown undermined his prospects to a crippling extent. In a few short months an ultra-confident teenager with instinctive natural skill at just about every ball game turned into a depressed and at times bitter young man, betrayed by stars he had admired from afar. It was very much a case of too much too soon.

'I desperately wanted someone to give me advice, to tell me about first-class cricket and to explain what the tour was all about,' he admits. 'When I set out I couldn't imagine how

43

Brian Close, his face revealing the intensity of his concentration, forces the ball away through the offside.

much misery the trip to Australia would bring and I'm sure that it left a mark. I had a groin injury, but some of the other players thought I must be swinging the lead. That was ridiculous really. I wanted to play and do my best, but I just felt out of my depth. At times I seriously felt like killing myself.' Close had begun his Test career with nought against New Zealand at Old Trafford and in October 1949 the army called him up for National Service.

As a consequence he missed much of the 1950 season, so his preference over several experienced county cricketers for the much coveted Australian tour may not have gone down too well with some of the senior professionals who regarded him as a pampered upstart. At the time, Close expressed his own surprise, saying: 'As I have not been free to play much first-class cricket I had lost all hope of being considered.'

It may be, too, that his approach ruffled a few feathers. His in-born talent had also brought him soccer recognition with Leeds United — he later signed for Arsenal — and he tended to be a bit brash. Bill Bowes, the father figure in Yorkshire cricket after the war, shrewdly observed: 'Brian never did as well as he could have done. It was not so much that he lacked ability, but because he was too confident. I would not call him big-headed. He knew what he could do and set out to do it. That confidence sometimes led him astray. He had an early lesson from Roly Jenkins, the great Worcestershire leg-spinner. In that first season at Worcester I asked Brian what he made of Jenkins. "Not much, I'll hit him over the pavilion," he replied. Sure enough, he did just that, but Jenkins waited, moved his field and Brian fell into the trap. A less confident, more thoughtful cricketer would have stored that experience away.

'I told Freddie Brown at the time that I did not agree with taking Close to Australia. He had too much to learn. I covered that tour as a journalist and saw for myself that Brian, as a non-smoking teetotaller, had energy to burn. He wanted to be on the move all the time and he could not understand why the older players were content to sit and enjoy a quiet drink while talking about the game. I appreciated that the last thing he would do was magnify an injury, but others on the tour did think him lazy. The opposite was the case, but some mud stuck and I am convinced that the whole business did so much harm.'

Significantly, Close did the double only once more, although, to put his career figures into perspective, no one ever made more sacrifices for the team. Few found themselves so easily in the centre of controversy. For a while Close attempted to develop as a professional footballer, moving from Arsenal, who released him, to Bradford City, where a serious knee injury persuaded him to concentrate his mind on cricket.

It would be fair to say that few sportsmen have matched the range of his achievements, for he has proved a brilliant golfer, getting a handicap of two left-handed and six right-handed. He could generally offer a generous start at billiards and snooker, was a great competitor at tennis and won trophies at boxing. He added to all this a respectable academic background, qualifying for a university place at seventeen, yet somehow he so often seemed to be at odds with the world.

Forthright, loyal, fearless and friendly, Close possibly aroused envy in too many hearts for his own good and his tendency to speak his mind must have given some offence. 'I am supposed to have been a controversial character and a lot would say I still am,' he acknowledges, 'but basically I am an easy going chap. The trouble may have been that I have principles and I have always stuck by them. This is a drawback in certain quarters and there have been times when I wished I were different, but I could not be two-faced and I cannot hide my true feelings.

'I have never been deliberately difficult with anyone, but if I took on a job I gave it top priority no matter what the cost. If I had to stick my neck out, so be it. I was ready to back up what I thought was right and I never did anyone a dirty trick.'

Undoubtedly these qualities made him a popular choice to succeed Vic Wilson as Yorkshire captain in 1963 and he led the county to four championships.

Looking back, Close appreciates his good fortune in taking over a team packed with experience and ability. 'We had some outstanding cricketers, men who could have walked into almost any team in the world like Fred Trueman, Ray Illingworth, Jimmy Binks and Tony Nicholson, in my opinion one of the best new-ball bowlers never to play for England. There were some strong personalities and the trick as captain was to get the best out of them as a unit.'

Yorkshire captured their second successive championship in his first year in charge and, after a couple of lean summers by their standards, were on top again in 1966, when Close received what amounted to an SOS from the Test selectors. The series against the West Indies developed along disastrous lines which were to become all-too familiar in the 1970s and '80s but which were not acceptable in the '60s. The tourists won by an innings and 40 runs at Old Trafford, by 139 runs at Trent

Bridge and by an innings and 55 runs at Headingley, where the captain, Colin Cowdrey, had his car damaged by irate spectators.

The only semblance of respectability was achieved at Lord's, where England gained an honourable draw and might have won with a slightly harder approach.

Two captains, Mike Smith and Cowdrey, had been tried by the time the final match loomed at the Oval and Close became the third. It was the first time England had changed horses in midstream with such confused regularity, but this time they had backed a winner. 'It was a tremendous honour and a heck of a challenge,' says Close. 'Morale had hit rock bottom and the first thing I had to do was to put some fight back into English cricket.' The selectors made six changes and England won by an innings and 34 runs. They bowled out West Indies for 268 only to slump to 166 for seven themselves, at which point the sorry pattern of the campaign seemed to be repeating itself.

Close, however, had already set a positive example, crouching aggressively at short-leg and silly mid-off and using his bowling shrewdly. The rest of the side picked up the mood of defiance and the remaining three wickets added an unbelievable 361 runs. Tom Graveney got 165 and John Murray 112, while the last pair, Ken Higgs and John Snow, dragged attention away from the start of another soccer season by putting on 128 in two hours as they broke the West Indies' spirit.

Garfield Sobers, at the height of his powers, stood as the only obstacle to England's victory and Close brilliantly outwitted his rival skipper, who had totally dominated the series up to that moment. As Sobers approached the wicket Close directed Snow to give him a bouncer first ball. The Sussex paceman followed his instructions to the letter, Sobers without taking time to judge the pace of the pitch, hooked and Close, waiting in the leg trap square to the wicket, held the catch. The rest became little more than a formality and praise showered on Close from all quarters.

'I was sure we would win after the first day when we bowled them out for only 268,' he claimed. 'We had so much good batting that someone had to come off. Graveney and Murray battled wonderfully well, but the last stand by Higgs and Snow came out of the blue. In earlier Tests the England fielding was not good, but in this one it was superb, probably because there were different players on duty. It was an easy side to handle. Everyone was willing to do anything asked of them. Possibly some players have found the difference between three-day championship cricket and five-day Tests a problem and they will need time to adjust, but the result confirms my contention that there is a lot of the right material in England.'

Subsequent events confirmed his opinions as India went down 3-0 and Pakistan 2-0 in 1967, leaving Close with a record of six wins and one draw from seven Tests, but, as is the case in so many areas of life, he fell out of favour in the sorriest of circumstances.

He ran into trouble at Edgbaston on August 18, 1967, as Yorkshire contrived to prevent Warwickshire scoring 142 to win the match in the last hour and forty minutes. In doing so they got through just twenty-four overs. Even worse, they unsuccessfully attempted to leave the field in the last fifteen minutes because of a shower and bowled two overs in that period, one from Trueman containing two no-balls and three bouncers.

The M.C.C. emergency committee investigated the circumstances and severely censured Close in a strongly worded statement which read: 'We came to the unanimous decision that the Yorkshire team used delaying tactics during the second Warwickshire innings and that these tactics constituted unfair play and were against the best interests of the game. Furthermore, the committee held the captain Brian Close entirely responsible for these tactics.' Despite this the Test selection committee, under the chairmanship of Doug Insole, from Essex, voted by four to two in favour of retaining Close as captain for the West Indies tour only to be overruled by the full

Two of the greatest all-rounders, Brian Close and West Indian Gary Sobers meet at Headingley.

M.C.C. committee. In view of his record, Close deserved better treatment.

The sense of injustice still rankles. 'I believe that some influential people at Lord's did not want me to take England to the West Indies because they were afraid I might speak out of turn. They intended to get rid of me if at all possible. There were those who thought I should have apologised in the hope of keeping the England captaincy and the whole business certainly cost me a lot, but I couldn't say I was sorry when I had nothing to be sorry about. I was doing my job for my county.

'There had been some complaints about the bowlers and fielders picking the seam of the ball in county matches, so the M.C.C., who controlled the game then, issued an instruction that the ball had to be dried in the presence of the umpire. Rain made the ground quite wet at Edgbaston and we needed to use the towel after every delivery. This slowed things down, but we could hardly be expected to operate with the ball like a bit of soap.

'In addition, I found it necessary to spread the field fairly deep which made communication difficult. It was my responsibility to put Yorkshire's interests first and that is exactly what I did. I was bitterly disappointed at the time and spent two of the worst weeks of my life waiting to see what they would do about the captaincy. In the end I lost it. I even arrived late at the enquiry as my car broke down and I had to thumb a lift, which sums up how things went for me.'

Close never got the chance to lead England again, although he answered his country's call with typical courage as a 45-year-old in 1976, when the West Indies' battery of fast bowlers were striking fear into the hearts of batsmen all over the world. He took them on without any thought for his own safety at a time when most of his contemporaries had settled for the comfort of an armchair while restricting their more physical activities to a walk down to the local.

The West Indies figure prominently in Close's career. He led Yorkshire to victory over them at Middlesbrough in 1963 and in the same year played one of the most famous innings in the history of Test cricket against them. It produced his best score at this level, 70, and brought him widespread respect and admiration. The scene, fittingly, was Lord's, where England required 234 to win against the hostile bowling of Wes Hall and Charlie Griffith. John Edrich, Micky Stewart and Ted Dexter were out by the time the total reached 31 and Cowdrey took a fearful blow which broke a bone just over his left wrist. He had to retire, Close taking his place, joining Ken Barrington, the dogged Surrey batsman, in a resolute partnership which restored the balance of the contest.

Bad light ended play for the day in the late afternoon and conditions were still grim when the action resumed after lunch next day. Hall and Griffith remained a formidable proposition on a pitch that offered encouragement throughout. Barrington went, but wicketkeeper Jim Parks and Fred Titmus, the Middlesex spinner, gave Close much-needed support as he grimly defended his wicket, taking many lifting deliveries deliberately on his body.

As he ran out of partners, Close adopted a different attitude, moving down the pitch to meet Hall and Griffith in an attempt to disrupt their rhythm. Any fast bowler of reasonable repute would react to such cavalier treatment and Hall and Griffith responded by increasing the quota of short stuff as they peppered the advancing batsman without mercy. Close's gamble came off for a while, but finally, aiming a big swing, he was caught at the wicket. England, with the handicapped Cowdrey returning to stand at the non-striker's end in the final over, earned a draw, the result being significantly over-shadowed by the arguments surrounding Close's effort.

Frank Worrell, the West Indies captain, considered that Close had made a mistake in taking so many risks, although he paid tribute to the spirit of the innings. Predictably ignoring the discomfort Close turned up at Bramall Lane for Yorkshire's match against Glamorgan with a body closely resembling a relief map of the moon, and the county masseur George Allock admitted that he had seen nothing like it in his life. The West Indian bowlers had left fourteen black, blue and red weals on his chest and shoulders and Close also nursed a painful wrist. 'I don't blame Hall and Griffith, I would have done just the same in their place, They were trying to stop me getting runs,' he said at the time.

He also dismissed the criticism of his unorthodox tactics. 'I didn't lose any sleep over it. My intention was to try to win the game and it didn't come off. I tried my best and I couldn't do more than that. I have been written off so many times that I just ignore what people say about the way I play.

'At one time so many people were having a go at me that I thought they must be right. I kept starting again from scratch. That was no good.

'It was the nearest thing to warfare you could get on a cricket field at Lord's, but that's the way I like it. I do better when the atmosphere is tense. I didn't worry too much about getting hit; that is part of the game and I have taken a lot of knocks in my time. One thing is certain, I will take a lot more before I am finished.

'Physical courage is easy. The point is that when I get emotional I just don't feel pain. I know I have been hit, of course, and I suppose it must hurt. Yet I don't feel it because I am so totally immersed in what I am doing. People who are afraid are the ones who think they are going to get hit or who think they are feeling pain. Mental courage is different. I get embarrassed by sympathy. It's sympathy that makes you soft. Out in the middle when you are batting you know exactly where you stand. Basically everyone is against you. I certainly don't regret my innings.' Typically, Close shrugged off his aches and pains to bowl twenty-five overs aginst Glamorgan, taking six for 55 in the first innings. He scored 61 and got through another sixteen overs to capture four for 19 as the Welshmen were defeated by ten wickets.

That triumph undoubtedly compensated to an extent for the disappointment at Lord's, particularly as he was in his first season as captain of Yorkshire, and he had the satisfaction of taking the county to the championship in their centenary year. Unfortunately, 1963 also marked the beginning of the limited-overs era with the introduction of the Gillette Cup. Close did not agree with one-day cricket and gave everyone who would listen the benefit of his opinion on the subject.

'Frankly I would not go very far to watch the sort of cricket served up in these games,' he said. 'They hold very little

A blow on the head was nothing to worry about for Brian Close as spectators celebrate the 1967 championship triumph at Harrogate.

interest for me.' Lord's, who were anxious to promote a competition they hoped would bring financial salvation, warned him about his conduct, but he continued to broadcast variations on a well worn theme. 'It is the same as asking golfers like Jack Nicklaus and Gary Player to go round a championship course in an hour and ten minutes. They would score badly because they would have to put the emphasis on speed rather than skill. It's the same in cricket. The player with ability can shape the three-day contest, but a one-day match makes the player do things he knows to be ridiculous.' He could not, however, turn the tide of events and eventually his wholehearted condemnation of what he called 'workshop cricket' caused Yorkshire to dispense with his services in 1970.

Overall, Yorkshire did reasonably well under Close. They fulfilled 249 first-class fixtures, winning 97, losing 39 and drawing 113. They also won the Gillette Cup twice, despite the captain's reservations about the value of the exercise, but there had been some warning signs and towards the end of his spell in charge a very fine side was breaking up.

Ray Illingworth departed in unsatisfactory circumstances in 1968. Fred Trueman retired in the same year. Inevitably, Yorkshire slipped down the table, from first to twelfth in 1969, when they lost more matches than they won for the first time since 1891. It was, although no one knew it at the time, a clear sign of things to come and, as they were to do so often in the future, the committee began to look around for someone to blame. In November, 1970, they picked on Close, citing his lack of enthusiasm for limited-overs competitions — the Sunday League came into being in 1969 — as one reason and his injury problems — he missed six championship and seven Sunday League engagements in the previous season — as another. Their decision stunned Close and the Yorkshire public.

He recalls: 'The news shook me. I had been with Yorkshire for twenty-two years and could hardly believe the way in which they dismissed me. I felt I had three or four good years left in me and proved it by going down to Somerset and playing again for England. I knew nothing about their intentions until I got a telephone call from the cricket chairman Brian Sellers asking me to report to the ground. There was no hint that it was about the captaincy. When I arrived they gave me two choices. Either I could resign or they would announce I was no longer captain.

'My first reaction was to say that if they felt about it that way I would resign. I asked them how long I had to think things over and Sellers told me that they would be issuing a statement one way or the other at 2.0 p.m. I went home and discussed it with my wife, Vivienne, and a close friend and I decided I would not resign because I did not want to break faith with all the people who had supported my testimonial during the same year. It would have looked as if I had taken their money and turned my back on them.

'Yorkshire told me I was being relieved of the captaincy because of my attitude to Sunday cricket. This did not make a lot of sense, though. I was perfectly prepared to play it because I realised it had a part in the future of the game and most county cricketers, including those in the Yorkshire dressing room, felt exactly the same. Yorkshire were not doing well in the Sunday League, but the results were not down to me and the county seemed to ignore our two Gillette Cup victories.'

By sacking Close, the Yorkshire committee sparked a major row, the forerunner of many more surrounding Geoff Boycott, who took over the captaincy. An Action Group was formed to challenge the administration, but Close went on his way to Somerset, where he poured his energy into putting that hitherto unconsidered county on the map. He had much to do with the development of Ian Botham as a match winning all-rounder as he gave Somerset cricket a much-needed sense of purpose.

He also scored a century against Yorkshire — 102 at Taunton in his first season in the West Country — but he took no satisfaction from the embarrassment of his former colleagues. 'I play for Somerset and do my best,' he said, 'but I am still a Yorkshireman at heart. Obviously it is nice to get a century against Yorkshire but you have qualms when it is against the county for which you have played for more than twenty years. I did not build myself up for the match, and I have been in pretty good form with Somerset. I have no bitterness towards Yorkshire cricket, although I am still disappointed at the way the committee treated me. I was pleased at the way the Yorkshire players applauded me when I got my hundred, I think they all wish me well, even if they cannot have wanted me to make quite so many runs at their expense. I suppose this innings might just make one or two people think about all that has happened.'

In time the wounds healed. Close served as a Test selector and, after being elected an honorary life member of Yorkshire, joined the committee as one of the three Bradford representatives, going on to take office as cricket chairman in a difficult political situation.

He played a leading role in the removal of Boycott from the dressing room and linked up with Bob Appleyard in pushing through the Cricket Academy project. Looking back, he says: 'Down the years I was accused of arguing with authority, of being stubborn, but I never argued with an umpire or a referee in my life. I did not set out to challenge the system, but if you just accept everything without question you never learn anything or get anywhere. I am the same now as I was then. If I examine the pros and cons and come to a decision I back my judgement and if I am convinced I am right nothing will shift me.

'There were some people on the committee, including Boycott, who wanted to establish the Cricket Academy at Headingley. We investigated fully the possibilities in Leeds and at Bradford's Park Avenue ground and came down in favour of the latter on the evidence we studied. It turned out to be a bit of a fight, but the committee backed us because we had the facts on our side.

'If I am proved wrong I am the first to admit it and apologise, but I will not bow to pressure. I respect people who have an opinion and who get involved, but I detest those who are two-faced in or out of sport. Controversy certainly affected my life and I suppose when I was a lot younger I began to get a bit of a chip on my shoulder, but that has worn off. Being on the Yorkshire committee is hard work when you have to earn a living, but I don't begrudge the hours I put in because cricket is in my blood and always will be.'

CAREER DETAILS

FOR ENGLAND (1949-76)

Close appeared in 22 Tests. He scored 887 runs for an average of 25.34. He claimed 18 wickets for an average of 29.55.

FOR YORKSHIRE (1949-70)

Close completed 709 innings and scored 22,650 runs for an average of 31.94. He hit 33 centuries with a highest score of 198 against Surrey in 1960. He completed 1,000 runs in a season 13 times, his best being 1,821 in 1961. He took 967 wickets at 24.29 runs each. He took 100 wickets in a season twice, his best being 114 in 1952.

IN FIRST-CLASS CRICKET (1949-86)

Close completed 1,052 innings and scored 34,994 runs for an average of 33.26. He hit 52 centuries. He claimed 1,171 wickets for an average of 26.42. He held 813 catches and completed one stumping.

CHAPTER FOUR

Fred Trueman

Yorkshire cricket has no great tradition of fast bowling. There was George Freeman, from Boroughbridge, who claimed 209 wickets at a miserly average of 9.97 between 1865 and 1880 and recorded the first two hat-tricks for the county in 1868. There was also Alan Hill, from Lascelles Hall, described by W. G. Grace at one time as the 'fastest and best bowler in England.' Bill Bowes injected pace and hostility into the Yorkshire attack, too, although his great ability found expression in extra bounce from his 6ft. 5in. and in skilful exploitation of the conditions. For the most part, Yorkshire relied on controlled, reliable, economical medium pace and an excess of spin for their regular success.

Fred Trueman, from Stainton, near Doncaster, arrived on the scene in the late 1940s as something of a novelty, therefore — an out-and-out fast bowler, paying little or no heed to accuracy — but he went on to earn the unchallenged ranking as the best in the country's long and distinguished history. He also earned an unwelcome notoriety as he featured prominently in thousands of stories which invented prodigious feats of womanising and drinking.

'If I had done only a fraction of all the things I am supposed to have done, I would have been dead at twenty-five,' he says. 'I was basically just an ordinary lad who loved playing cricket and I never fathomed out how all these tall tales grew up around me. The first one I remember claimed that I had been a miner and couldn't mix with other cricketers.

'In fact, I was born in the country, which gave me a love of wild life which stuck with me. They used to say that I turned up at the nets in flashy clothes with nude women on my ties, but my dad would have given me a thick ear if I had. I suppose the most famous bit of fiction relates to the 1953 tour to the West Indies when I am supposed to have asked a VIP at an official dinner to "pass the salt Gunga Din." That is rubbish, for as a junior player I never got near the top table and the more important dignitaries.

'On another occasion, a Bristol hotel made a complaint about me when Yorkshire were playing Gloucestershire. Unfortunately for them I happened to be at Lord's representing England at the time, one hundred and fifty miles away. People always reckoned I spent most of my spare time swilling beer and chasing women, but nothing could be further from the truth. I usually went to my room and kept myself to myself. When I retired it was said that I had changed. Actually I remained exactly the same.'

Trueman enjoyed no easy entry into the first-class game. The fourth of seven children, he came from a hard-working background and owed much to his father, Allan Thomas, who encouraged him when the going got tough. Two school teachers at Maltby Hall Modern School, Tommy Stubbs and Dick Harrison, also steered him along the right road as a boy. He survived the trauma of being hit a very serious blow in the groin by a cricket ball and for eighteen months, which took in two cricket seasons, he had to attend Rotherham Hospital for treatment. The injury left no mental scars, nor any fear of being hurt again.

In those days, there were comparatively few really quick bowlers about at any level and the persistent physical intimidation, which is second nature to the West Indians, was unknown. Trueman, however, fired away and his natural rhythm enabled him to frighten out a lot of batsmen. There have been many misguided attempts, one involving Ted Dexter, to turn athletes into pacemen, the theory being that the right training can channel physical dexterity into a productive area for bowling. The results have been disastrous because genuine pace is God-given. Trueman's body slipped into the perfect cartwheel, with eyes peering down the pitch from outside the leading left arm, from the start. His successes inevitably carried him into the Sheffield schools' senior team and the Yorkshire boys. The next step took him to the county nets.

Bowes, as the bowling coach, placed the emphasis on developing pace, ensuring that Trueman did not suffer from being put under too much strain. 'A bowler has to strive for the extra yard of pace or he will not find it,' Bowes said. 'Genuine quick bowling is probably the most demanding of sporting activities and delivering the bouncer takes a lot out of the most mature bowler. We worked all along on the theory that speed was of the essence and that control could be added later.'

Trueman made his debut against Cambridge University in May, 1949, alongside Brian Close and Frank Lowson, a stylish opener destined to play for England. Trueman had not appeared for the Colts at that time, so he enjoyed a rare distinction in that sense and his progress was almost as rapid as his bowling. In his second season he had fourteen first-class appearances and earned a place in the Test trial. For some strange reason the authorities staged it at Bradford Park Avenue, calling up Trueman to give the senior batsmen, due to face the West Indies, practice against fast bowling. Trueman made the most of the situation by bowling his hero, Len Hutton, but ironically Jim Laker made a nonsense of the contest by taking eight wickets for two runs with his off-breaks. Later in the summer, spinners Sonny Ramadhin and Alf Valentine led the tourists to a 3-1 triumph in the Test series.

Although making his way impressively, Trueman noted: 'The dressing room in the 1950s was not an easy place. The team tended to split into little cliques with Hutton and the

In action for Lincoln City, Fred Trueman scored four goals for the A team on his debut against Appleby Frodingham in 1952.

captain Norman Yardley going their way and even staying in a different hotel to the rest of us. Youngsters like me could easily be left out in the cold and this applied equally at international level.' At the same time, Trueman responded to the thoughtful guidance of Yardley, who used him sympathetically.

'My happiest days at cricket were under Yardley,' he stresses. 'Norman knew so much about cricket he was able to give advice and help. He kept you interested by suggesting you tried this method or that to get a batsman out. After him, I rate Ronnie Burnet highly. He understood me and quickly appreciated that I was a lot more sensitive than anyone realised. I certainly worried if I had a bad day and he would always say the right thing to put matters into perspective.'

For his part, Yardley respected Trueman's great ability. 'He relied entirely on speed in the early days,' he said. 'It would never occur to him to slip in the yorker once he had got a batsman on the backfoot with a shorter deliver. The sight of the slightest apprehension at the other end persuaded him to try and bowl faster and shorter, but gradually he took notice and in his later years he had a tremendous facility for running through the late order. This can be a lot more difficult than spectators imagine.'

Trueman burst onto the Test scene against the hapless Indians in 1952. He had claimed thirty-one wickets in 1949 at 23.2 each and another thirty-one at 28.2 in 1950 before jumping to ninety at only 20.5 in 1951. He completed his first hat-trick against Nottinghamshire in that summer in the midst of a return of eight for 53 and it is interesting to note that only George Macaulay equalled his tally of four hat-tricks for the county. Coincidentally, Nottinghamshire were on the receiving end on three occasions with M.C.C. 'enjoying' the benefit of his attentions in the other case. As he departed for National Service with the RAF in the autumn of 1951, Trueman was comforted by the awarding of his county cap, then far more than now the seal of official approval, and the Test selectors were soon to be seeking his release for the series in the following summer.

He sensationally reduced the tourists to panic-stricken mediocrity, starting on the familiar Headingley ground where the old scoreboard revealed India at four wickets for no runs in their second innings, three of them having fallen to Trueman. 'I was on duty in the stores at RAF Hemswell in Lincolnshire when Yardley, as chairman of Selectors, rang to ask for my release,' he recalls. 'The station commander, Group Captain Warfield, said I could go if he got a couple of tickets for his wife and himself. He got them all right and I collected seven

The perfect action. Fred Trueman as the batsmen saw him.

wickets. I couldn't really believe that Test batsmen were backing away so far, but they showed me so much of the stumps that all I had to do was keep the ball straight.'

Trueman actually did nothing special in the first innings, finishing with three for 89 in a total of 293 from the football stand end. Headingley has a pronounced slope from the Kirkstall Lane end which can make life tricky for bowlers with long runs. Trueman had got used to operating down the slope which might well have been why he experienced some problems with his back foot, being 'no-balled' too often for comfort for dragging. When Hutton, England's first professional captain in his first match, switched him in the second innings he destroyed the Indians.

The famous score of four for none has cemented the Headingley Test into the brickwork of legend, but Trueman actually did better at Old Trafford, where his eight for 31 represented the best return by a genuine fast bowler in any international match. 'I think the Indians were beaten before they started,' he suggests. 'They definitely did not like the quick stuff and Hutton made the most of their anxiety. I bowled from the Stretford End and he gave me three slips, three gullies, silly point and two short legs. Brilliant catching added to the difficulties for the Indians and they just gave up the ghost.'

Trueman completed the four-match series with a haul of twenty-nine wickets at 13.31 runs each as England triumphed by three games to nil, and at the end of the campaign he reluctantly put on one side his hopes of becoming a soccer star, too. He attracted the attention of Lincoln City while playing in the RAF and turned out for their Midland League side. Yardley, in his dual role as captain of Yorkshire and chairman of the England selectors, shared a widespread anxiety that Trueman might injure himself and be lost, at least on a temporary basis, to cricket. 'I realised that Norman had my best interests at heart and that, much as I liked soccer, I had to think about cricket first,' says Trueman.

It is one of the regrets of Trueman's life that he managed only one Test against Australia in 1953, when England regained the Ashes, and missed the 1954-55 trip, in the course of which they defended them successfully. 'I did not have a great time in the West Indies in the winter of 1953-54, with only nine wickets at 46.6 runs each and I reckoned that the matting wickets out there cut two or three years out of my life,' he reflects. 'Strangely I had a few arguments with Len Hutton on that trip and I thought at the time that they cost me my place in Australia. He told me he wanted me but was over-ruled. Anyway, 1954 turned out to be a disappointment. I had my best figures of eight for 28 against Kent at Dover, but didn't appear in the series with Pakistan and then found myself out in the cold during the winter.'

England's 3-1 success overshadowed the arguments about

Comrades in arms. Brian Close and Fred Trueman plan a few surprises for the opposition.

the touring party, but Trueman could count himself unlucky. Hutton, having endured some painful moments at the hands of Ray Lindwall and Keith Miller, understandably put the emphasis on pace. Brian Statham, top of the county averages, and Alec Bedser, fifth, demanded selection, although the latter figured in only one Test, but Trueman, in ninth place, lost out to Frank Tyson, the Northamptonshire man who emerged as the key figure.

Trueman tended to ruffle a few feathers. 'I've always believed in speaking my mind and that is why I found myself in hot water from time to time. I have never been one to sit back and let things happen if I thought they were wrong. I shouted up when I spotted what I regarded as a fault in anything. There were rows between Closey and me when he was captain, but we respected each other. Getting things out in the open is much better than letting them fester. All the same, I probably missed playing in about thirty Tests because some people in the MCC were set against me.'

He felt cheated again in 1956 when overlooked for the tour to South Africa — 'I never did play a Test out there' — but his wicket-taking efficiency guaranteed him a stream of international calls, despite fierce competition. The first-class averages for 1965, for example, make fascinating reading for a generation accustomed to the sight of England scratching around for anyone who can propel the ball roughly in the right direction at any sort of decent speed. The listing included:

Harold Rhodes (Derbyshire) 119 wickets at 11.04

Brian Jackson (Derbyshire) 120 at 12.42

Brian Statham (Lancashire) 137 at 12.52

Tom Cartwright (Warickshire) 108 at 13.93

Trueman 127 at 14.25

Jack Flavell (Worcestershire) 142 at 14,78

David Larter (Northants) 87 at 15.32

Jeff Jones (Glamorgan) 84 at 15.90

Derek Shacketon (Hampshire) 144 at 16.08.

All of these seamers were operating in a championship of twenty-eight matches and every one of them would clearly have walked into any side of the 1980s. By that summer, however, Trueman had made a major entry in the record books by becoming the first man to take 300 Test wickets.

His outstanding effort came at Headingley in July 1961, when he captured eleven wickets for 88 runs and, in the course of two devastating spells, destroyed the Australians. Largely under his influence England swept to victory by eight wickets with two days to spare. Trueman exploited a controversial pitch of uneven bounce to maximum effect, although it is interesting to note that the tourists had reached a comfortable-looking 183 for two on the first day when he took a destructive hand for the first time. Trueman ripped out the heart of the innings in six hostile overs, claiming five for 16, but England had to apply themselves carefully to gain a slender 62-run first-innings lead.

Down the pavilion steps at Park Avenue, Bradford, marches Fred Trueman and there is a sparkle of anticipation in the eyes of the spectators.

Australia wiped out their arrears and had reached 98 for two when, at 3.40 on the Saturday afternoon, Peter May, the England captain, decided to change the bowling. He might well have had it in the back of his mind to merely switch the spinners, but Trueman, recalled to the attack, decided to try a little experiment of his own. Cutting down his run and his pace, he bowled little off-cutters. Norman O'Neill nudged a single in his first over, but Trueman then took five wickets without conceding another run. Neil Harvey was caught for 53, O'Neill for 19. Ken Mackay edged to the wicketkeeper, Bobby Simpson and Benaud were also caught and, for good measure, Trueman accounted for Alan Davidson, too. Eight Australian wickets fell for 28 altogether in one of Test cricket's most spectacular collapses.

Interestingly, Harold Jackson, of Derbyshire, who took over one hundred wickets season after season, played the second of his two Tests, a meagre ration which emphasised there were a lot of very good seam bowlers about in the '60s.

The Australians provided the oppositions at the Oval in 1964 and the game involved a series of statistical milestones. Colin Cowdrey completed 5,000 runs for England, Ken Barrington got to 4,000 and Geoff Boycott scored the first of his twenty-two Test centuries. All of these achievements were, however, eclipsed by Trueman's record. He had 297 victims to his credit when he started the game on August 13 and, strangely, both he and Cowdrey were celebrating a recall to international duty after being dropped for the fourth Test.

It had been a low-key series, pot-marked by bad weather and injuries. Fred Titmus, the Middlesex offspinner, earned a footnote in the story of Boycott's life and times by featuring as his opening partner in an emergency at Trent Bridge. England, having been beaten by seven wickets at Headingley, needed to win at the Oval to square the series, but they never looked likely to manage that after being bowled out for 182, with Neil Hawke taking six for 47. The Australians made a solid, functional reply. Being in such a position of strength, they saw no need to hurry.

As the contest drifted along, Ted Dexter, the England captain, appeared to have lost interest. 'With about ten minutes to go to lunch, I suspected that he was going to try something unorthodox like putting on Peter Parfitt with his supposed spinners,' Trueman recalls. 'I couldn't allow that, so I literally put myself on, grabbing the ball and marking out my short run. I suppose it amounted to a bit of insubordination, but I got away with it and promptly got one to cut back off the seam to bowl Ian Redpath. Graham McKenzie came in next and he edged the first delivery to slip, where Cowdrey held the catch, so there I was on 299 wickets with the prospect of a hat-trick.'

One of Fred Trueman's greatest moments in cricket involved captaining Yorkshire to victory over the Australians in 1968. Here he leads on the side at Headingley for a championship game.

No dramatist could have embellished the scene, for as McKenzie returned to the pavilion, the umpires decided that luncheon would be taken. The spectators suffered agonies of frustration and expectation, but Trueman remained fairly calm throughout. 'I just sat there having a cup of tea thinking about that 300th wicket and wondering if I would collect my fifth hat-trick. I didn't eat much lunch, but I felt certain that the wicket would come, so I can't say that I was worried. The next man in was a really good mate of mine, Neil Hawke, who, at the back of his mind, realised that he would earn a bit of fame by becoming my 300th victim.'

After all the tension of the long, dragging minutes of the interval, the first ball on the resumption proved to be very much an anti-climax as it sped well wide of the offstump through to the wicketkeeper without Hawke having to take much notice. He actually made 14 and Trueman was beginning to run out of a bit of steam before an edge to Cowdrey, still at slip, ended all anxieties.

Trueman got to the 300 mark in sixty-five Tests with a striking rate of four and a half wickets per game. His appearances had been distributed over thirteen years. The rash of international cricket which spread across the world in the 1980s devalued so many statistics, pushing the great names of the past into the background. Even so, by 1990 only Ian Botham and Bob Willis had overtaken Trueman in the list of English wicket-takers, the former with 397 from ninety-seven matches and the latter with 325 from ninety. Among the world stars Malcolm Marshall, from the West Indies, Australian Dennis Lillee and Richard Hadlee, the backbone of the New Zealand attack, rank alongside Trueman in terms of striking rate, but for him the man who commands most respect is Ray Lindwall, the great Australian. 'He took 228 wickets at 23.03,' says Trueman without needing to turn to any reference book, 'and he was the best.'

Close believes that Trueman's greatest strength was simply that 'he wanted to bowl fast', and he had the aggressive streak that caused batsmen so much concern. His forthright approach also led him into dispute with the Yorkshire authorities from time to time. Captain Vic Wilson sent him home from Taunton in 1962 when he arrived late to the ground, a decision which Trueman thought at the time very harsh. The committee also took exception to his initial excursions into journalism while still a player, and in August 1965 his apparent refusal to accept Close's tactics in the Roses clash with Lancashire brought suspension and a stern warning from cricket chairman Brian Sellers.

Happily, however, the troubles always blew over, for, warts and all, Trueman was irreplaceable. Even in troubled 1965 he had the satisfaction of captaining Yorkshire in the absence of Close and his finest hour in that direction came in 1968, his last year with the county, as he led them to victory over the Australians at Bramall Lane.

Yorkshire made a laboured 355 for nine, Trueman extending the innings as long as he dared into a gloomy second day. With the famous old ground fringed with low black cloud and thunder, Yorkshire whittled their way through the tourists' resistance, driven on by the acting captain's refusal to contemplate anything other than success. His own contribution amounted to six wickets for 83 as the team responded and Australia were defeated by an innings and 69 runs. 'That was the greatest moment of my career,' he insists. 'Obviously taking 300 Test wickets was something special, but I wanted to beat the Australians more than I had ever wanted anything in cricket. Yorkshire had not defeated them since 1902 and usually the county's game against them were regarded as extra Tests with a lot at stake. Hardly had we got off the field when a storm broke and the centre of Sheffield was awash within a few minutes.'

Like most bowlers, Trueman also enjoyed batting. He had a distinct advantage over others in that no one was ever likely to drop one short to him. The ultimate threat of reprisals made him safe so he could get on the front foot with a fair amount of confidence. He tended to give the ball a healthy thump, but he could defend skilfully and resolutely when the occasion demanded and, as Close observes: 'Fred was a much better batsman than most people gave him credit for. If he had not been so important as a bowler he might well have made a lot more runs. He possessed a decent range of strokes.'

Trueman managed two championship centuries — 104 against Northamptonshire in 1963 and 101 against Middlesex in 1965 — and he also held many fine catches at short leg. 'He was very sloppy in the field in his first season or so,' says Close, 'but he finished up as a brilliant catcher close to the wicket and with a wonderful arm from the deep. Nobody took any liberties when he had the ball anywhere near his hand.'

Trueman retired in November 1968. 'It was a sad day,' he confirms. 'I had so many happy memories and money certainly had nothing to do with it. I felt I had a couple of good years left in me and I did help out Derbyshire briefly, but I wanted to go out at the top.'

Yorkshire having made him an honorary life member, he served on the committee as the representative for the Craven district, becoming embroiled in the turmoil surrounding Geoff Boycott. The political strife, sadly, ended his association with the county. An outspoken critic of Boycott's influence on the team, he lost his place on the committee to Peter Fretwell, a printer, in the 1984 resolution and he resolutely turned his back on the club. 'I gave thousands of hours to Yorkshire cricket and spent hundreds of pounds of my own money trying to put them back at the top. I even offered at one stage to come out of retirement to help out,' he says.

'When the members decided they did not want me on the committee, I thought it was time to give up. However, it hurts me to see Yorkshire trailing along with the also-rans. They seemed to lack the will to go all out for victory in the 1980s. My main asset was a real determination which stemmed from my background. Material things were in short supply so you had to fight for what you wanted.'

The difference between Fred Trueman and other great bowlers of the post-war era, such as Alec Bedser and Brian Statham, and the modern seamers is that they stayed fit. Trueman got through 1,068 overs in 1960, 1,190 in the following year and 1,141 in 1962, a sequence well beyond the physical scope of most modern counterparts. 'I don't think all this general training does much good,' he argues. 'I prepared myself just by bowling. That is the only way to build up the right muscles. I started in the nets steadily bowling a few overs at a gentle pace, and gradually increased the tempo. We were lucky, I suppose, in having matches against Oxford and Cambridge Universities and, usually, MCC before getting down to the serious business of the championship, so I had plenty of opportunity to make sure I was in great shape. Nowadays it's straight into some one-day game or other.'

As first-class cricket charts an uncertain course through troubled financial and political waters, it seems very unlikely that the system will produce another Trueman. He was, without doubt a unique talent.

CAREER DETAILS

FOR ENGLAND (1952-65)

Trueman appeared in 67 Tests. He took 307 wickets at 21.57 runs each. His best figures were eight for 31 against India at Old Trafford in 1952. He scored 981 runs for an average of 13.81.

FOR YORKSHIRE (1949-68)

Trueman took 1,745 wickets at 17.13. He claimed 100 wickets on eight occasions, his best being 150 in 1960. He completed 452 innings and scored 6,852 runs for an average of 15.15.

IN FIRST-CLASS CRICKET (1949-69)

Trueman took 2,304 wickets at 18.29. He completed 593 innings and scored 9,232 runs for an average of 15.56. He held 438 catches.

CHAPTER FIVE

Bob Appleyard

Bob Appleyard was something of a freak, a once-in-a-lifetime bowler of infinite variety and resource. He appeared for Yorkshire between 1950 and 1958, but missed the 1952 and 1953 seasons because of lung trouble which required major surgery and he did not make his England debut until his thirtieth year. He stands no higher than twenty-fifth in Yorkshire's list of wicket-takers with 637 and claimed only 31 Test victims, yet Bill Bowes, who played with arguably the county's strongest side in the 1930s and for England from 1932 to 1946, rated him in the top three bowlers he had seen, the other two being Australian Bill O'Reilly and Staffordshire's legendary S.F. Barnes.

Even more than Wardle, with whom he formed such a devastating county association, Appleyard represented two bowlers in one. He delivered medium-paced inswingers with the new ball and added quite brisk offspin once the shine had gone. Throughout he operated from a run of around sixteen yards, using his considerable height — 6ft. 1in. — to add unpleasant bounce. 'I always thought that using a fairly long run was important,' he says. 'It enabled me to change pace without giving too many clues to the batsmen. On the flattest of pitches a bowler can cause problems by varying his speed and flight and the trouble with so much cricket in the 1970s and '80s was that the medium-paced trundlers sent down over after over for all counties were identical. Batsmen did not have to think or worry about what might be coming next.'

Appleyard was a relatively late developer, first playing for Yorkshire as a twenty-five-year-old, but this proved something of an advantage, for he emerged from a hard and demanding apprenticeship with Bowling Old Lane in the Bradford League more than ready for the challenge that lay ahead.

In his early days he showed most promise as a batsman, but on moving to Priestman Central School, Bradford, as a twelve-year-old he began to take bowling more seriously. He did well enough to gain the captaincy of Bradford Boys and, in the final of the Yorkshire elementary schools' competition, took five Sheffield Boys' wickets for as many runs in a total of 22. Surprisingly in a county which prided itself — and still does — on giving a priority to the finding and nurturing of youthful talent, Appleyard didn't catch the official eye for a considerable time. In 1950 he had a remarkable return of 41.2 overs, 13 maidens, 63 runs and 15 wickets for the second team against Staffordshire, going on to head the Colts' averages, yet no one appears to have enthused about his potential. His calm, solid temperament allowed him to continue in league cricket without complaint.

'There were many very good players in the Bradford League and I learned a lot before moving on to county cricket,' he says. This goes a long way towards explaining why he captured a record haul of 200 wickets in his first full season. Like every other 'overnight sensation', he had prepared thoroughly.

In measuring the magnitude of that achievement, it is important to note that the previous highest haul had been 154 by Wilfred Rhodes in 1898 and, with the changing pattern of the county game, it is safe to say that no one is likely to come close to doing better than Appleyard.

He made his debut against Surrey at the Oval on July 22, 1950, when acting captain Don Brennan lost the toss. The home side duly took first use of what by general consent was a very good batting pitch and Yorkshire, with a weakened attack, braced themselves for a long day in the field. Appleyard shared the new ball with Alec Coxon and exceeded his highest expectations by taking three for 18 in his first spell. He remembers the occasion clearly.

'Although exclusively a seam bowler in those days, I had been shown how to produce the offspinner by Stanley Douglas, a very good league cricketer who took forty-nine wickets for Yorkshire as an occasional choice in the late 1920s and early '30s. After bowling steadily for a short while, I suddenly decided to try an offspinner. Happily I dropped it right on the spot and Fletcher, the Surrey opener, had an enormous swipe at it, missed and was bowled. I then did Peter May with the same ball for a duck, although at that stage no one in the Yorkshire camp actually knew I could spin the ball.'

Appleyard had another advantage in addition to his height. He was blessed with very big hands and strong fingers which enabled him to give the ball a genuine tweak. 'I went into engineering as an apprentice at fifteen,' he explains. 'One of my jobs initially involved hammering to trim toughened steel and this exercise did a lot to strengthen my hands and particularly the fingers on my right hand.'

He did not earn selection for the first match of the historic 1951 season and Yorkshire took a thrashing from the M.C.C. batsmen at Lord's. They conceded a total of 411 for seven declared as Fred Trueman, Bill Foord, Vic Wilson, Norman Yardley, Eddie Leadbeater and Wardle toiled in vain. Changes for the next engagement with Oxford University in the Parks brought Appleyard his chance and he took it with four for 26 in a rain-ruined draw. This added up to a significant performance as Yorkshire knew they would lack the services of Coxon, who had moved into league cricket, and Brian Close, then regarded as the first-choice offspinner.

Once Appleyard had slipped into the groove, he compensated for the absence of both men, showing tremendous stamina and resolve. As Bowes, by then reporting on cricket

Bob Appleyard, one of the most respected bowlers in the world when at the height of his powers.

for the *Yorkshire Evening News*, observed: 'With such a fine utility bowler at their disposal Yorkshire suffered from the temptation to give him too much work. By acting as both seamer and spinner, he allows them to play an extra batsman, but it would be a tragedy if he were to be handicapped by bowling too many overs.'

Appleyard actually got through 1,313 overs to take his 200 wickets for 2,829 runs at an average of 14.14. Discounting West Indian Sonny Ramadhin, who had fourteen wickets for 90 runs, he stood at the head of the first-class averages, poised, to all intents, on the verge of a truly great career. He had demonstrated a capacity for learning, even when things were going so well for him. He noticed, for example, that Len Hutton, at slip, usually moved deeper as he ran in to bowl his quicker ball as an offspinner. 'I reasoned that, if he knew, the batsmen might well get some idea, so I asked him how he spotted what I intended,' says Appleyard. 'He told me that I held the ball differently, so I worked on that privately.'

Appleyard also began spinning the ball off his middle finger and discovered that he had more control. 'That came about by accident,' he recalls. 'I was doing so much bowling that my forefinger became sore and blistered so I switched to give it a rest and it worked very well.' By mid-June Appleyard had taken 77 wickets and attracted a lot of attention. 'He has become shock-bowler, stock bowler and wicket taker in chief,' commented the *Yorkshire Evening Post*.

'Obviously I was very happy with my success,' says Appleyard, 'but I found it very hard work and it was a good job I was a very fit man. I didn't really think about taking 200 wickets or anything like that. We were involved in the championship race, as usual, and eventually finished second to Warwickshire, so it was always a case of what was best for the side. As Yorkshiremen we wanted to win and no one ever thought for one second of holding back so that I could take wickets. It simply did not work like that. Johnny Wardle, for instance, wanted every wicket he could take and Trueman was trying to force his way into the England side. We were a united team, but each individual tried hard for himself, too. One problem for me was that Johnny got through his overs so quickly, especially when the batsmen were on the defensive. Sometimes he would complete an over in a minute, so I hardly had time to draw breath before I found myself back in action.'

Appleyard in action at the nets at Headingley.

The Scarborough Festival, at the height of its popularity, provided entertaining cricket with a serious undertone. Players used the occasion to relax at the end of the serious business and looked to collect the odd runs or wickets they needed to reach 1,000 or 100, but Appleyard arrived at the splendid North Marine Road ground in September 1951 with a mammoth task on his hands. 'I needed eleven wickets for 200,' he says. 'By that stage, of course, the target was very much in mind, but I had been picked for only the one game — Yorkshire v M.C.C., so I felt that the odds must be against me.'

He quickly shifted the balance of probability in his favour by claiming eight wickets in the first innings for 76, but after that the situation became distinctly complicated. He soon removed his 198th victim when M.C.C. batted a second time on the last day, Bill Edrich, of Middlesex and England, being safely held by Hutton on the long-on boundary. Appleyard bowled on, spurred on by an enthusiastic crowd and an inner conviction that the most difficult part of the job had been accomplished. M.C.C. were in no mood to surrender, however, and they resisted stubbornly.

Commonsense dictated that, despite his obvious reluctance to come off, he had to take the occasional rest. Trueman and Wardle enjoyed some success while he fretted in the outfield and then rain cut forty minutes out of the proceedings. Eventually M.C.C. had only two wickets standing and Appleyard needed them both. 'It was a pretty tense situation,' he confesses. 'Every ball counted and I had to make sure that I didn't lose control.' He took his two wickets in one over amidst scenes of wild excitement. Derbyshire's Tom Hall drove firmly to Normal Yardley at mid-on off the first ball, the captain showing his relief at holding the catch by fanning his face with his cap. 'It was not a particularly difficult catch, but I must admit I reflected on what might have happened had I dropped it,' he said afterwards as the celebrations gathered momentum. Roy Tattersall, the Lancashire offspinner and left-handed batsman, safely negotiated three deliveries before holing out to Trueman, also at mid-on. 'I suppose the general feeling of suspense did get to me a bit, says Appleyard, 'but I think that the fielders crouching for so long in the leg trap must have felt worse. There was a great sense of relief when it was all over and, after the elation, sheer fatigue weighed me down. It had been hard going in my first full season and I was glad when it was all over.'

As Wardle observed: 'It was a bit like having both Alec Bedser and Jim Laker in your team and Bob was probably the most dangerous bowler in the country at that time.' Possibly the efforts of that long, hard summer took too much out of even his strong frame, for Appleyard became ill in May the following year. The initial diagnosis was pleurisy which became tuberculosis and he had half of one lung removed. Recovery was inevitably a long, slow process, taking in a spell at a Swiss clinic, and two years elapsed before he returned to first-class cricket.

'In many ways I am very lucky to be alive,' he concedes. 'A few years earlier I might well have died, for medical science had made important strides in the treatment of tuberculosis. Playing cricket again was a bonus. I had put on a stone in weight during my illness, but I got tired easily and knew I would have to work hard to build myself up again. Luckily, they had constructed an indoor cricket shed at Manningham Mills which provided a pretty long run-up, so I could practise almost as much as I liked.'

He put the facility to excellent use and marked his reappearance against Somerset at Taunton in 1954 by taking seven for 16 in the second innings. The home side were dismissed for 48 and Appleyard had plundered his seven wickets in one spell for four runs from twenty-seven balls to give him match figures of twelve for 88. His form remained admirable, bringing him the first of his nine Test caps against Pakistan that summer.

Few bowlers have arrived on the international scene in quite such spectacular fashion. When acting captain David Shepherd called Appleyard into the attack, Pakistan had made a solid enough start, but the Yorkshireman turned the game on its head. His second delivery beat the great Hanif Mohammad to bring a clear-cut lbw decision, while Godfrey Evans held the catch which removed Maqsood Ahmed in Appleyard's third over. The first ball of the fourth over and the second of the fifth brought further successes.

Waqar Hassan and Imtiaz Ahmed were both bowled, the latter having his offstump sent flying. Appleyard claimed four for six in twenty-six balls, and he is one of the few bowlers to record his best Test figures in his first innings, but did not play for England again that summer because of injury.

Even so, he earned an unchallenged place in Hutton's party for the tour to Australia with 154 first-class wickets at 14.42 runs each. 'Obviously I was very pleased with both my form and fitness, although I got tired quickly and had to push myself at times, he says. He actually bowled 1,026 overs, so he had every reason to feel a bit weary, and no modern bowler would fancy being saddled with such a heavy workload even though so much attention is paid to fitness. 'Once you have been seriously ill, you wonder how you are going to manage, whether everything will be all right,' he points out. 'I experienced some difficulty in getting my breath, which was not surprising as I had lost half of one lung, but I put the doubts to the back of my mind and tried to forget them. Being picked for England and doing well obviously acted as a tremendous tonic.'

England's triumph over Australia during the winter of 1954-55 was the first 'Down Under' since the famous 'body-line' series of 1932-33 and it meant that the Ashes were retained for the first time in nearly thirty years. There is no doubt that Frank Tyson represented Hutton's main strike force, for the Northamptonshire fast bowler claimed twenty-eight wickets at 20.82 to earn himself a permanent place in cricket's Hall of Fame. His explosive pace shattered Australian confidence and the shrewd Hutton used him brilliantly, but the fact remains that Appleyard headed the bowling averages with eleven victims at 20.36.

He did not play in the first Test at Brisbane, where England, having elected to field first, lost by an innings and 154 runs, but he subsequently did a magnificent job in balancing the attack. Firstly, however, he had to dispel the lingering fears about his fitness. 'I recall an early match on the tour when I really thought I might not be able to make a significant contribution,' he admits. 'We had had a long day in the field and I hardly had the strength to walk off at the end.

An imposing trio of golfers. Johnny Wardle (left), Brian Close and Bob Appleyard were all very useful players with low handicaps.

Then I looked around the dressing room and realised that all the team were in the same position, including those who had not bowled. The heat had sapped everybody's strength and I realised I had nothing to worry about.

He still regards the Adelaide Test, the fourth, in January of 1954 as his most memorable match. 'We arrived at the beautiful Oval there leading by two games to one with the chance to win the series,' he says, adding: 'We all knew that if we lost we were back where we started, so the team were all keyed up. It proved an extremely tense contest from start to finish, played in a temperature of almost 100 degrees.

'I also endured a very embarrassing moment. Australia won the toss and, after being 229 for eight at one time, staged a determined recovery. Len Maddocks, the wicketkeeper, and Ian Johnston put on 92 and made things very difficult for us. With the score at 278, Maddocks called for a run and was sent back rather belatedly by his partner. I fielded the ball at short mid-wicket and, with both batsmen at the bowler's end, all I had to do was throw it to wicketkeeper Godfrey Evans.

'Taking careful aim I threw what I intended to be a slow lob which would make an easy catch, but, to my horror, the ball rose high over the head of Evans to be taken in the slips by Colin Cowdrey. We missed such an easy run out and I never did fathom just what went wrong. It must have had something to so with the timing of the throw, just as a slowly played golf shot can sometimes travel a tremendous distance.

'Happily I got the chance to redeem myself in the Australian second innings after we had gained a lead of 18, with Len making top score of 80 and Colin 79. There was some solid batting right down the order and I finished with ten not out. Australia batted again late on the fourth day and in the last over before tea I caught and bowled their opener Arthur Morris, who had been involved in an unfortunate accident.

'He chopped the ball into the ground and it bounced to gully, where it hit Cowdrey and broke his nose. I think Morris might have lost his concentration because I took his wicket with the next delivery. In the evening session I bowled Jimmy Burke and Neil Harvey, the three wickets costing me six runs and, taking everything into account, I suppose that was about the best spell of bowling in my career.

Appleyard did not get the chance to finish off the Australians the next morning, even though his introduction into the attack had been hailed as a stroke of genius on the part of Hutton. The captain's faith in the speed of Tyson and Lancashire's Brian Statham was fully justified as the home side were dismissed for 111.

'Although we required only 94 to win, no one relaxed in our dressing room,' admits Appleyard. 'That great all-rounder Keith Miller removed Hutton, Bill Edrich and Cowdrey in the space of twenty balls. Peter May drove a catch to cover and England were 49 for four. Very few players could bear to watch and we stood at the back of the dressing room, Hutton included, waiting for verbal information and trying to interpret the noise made by the spectators. Eventually, with the score in the 70s we relaxed and saw the final stages.

'I found it difficult to sleep during the five days of the match. I kept bowling through the night as well as during the day, but there was a nice interlude when Don Bradman invited Cowdrey and myself to his home for dinner. I spent a fascinating evening listening to my boyhood hero talking about cricket.'

Appleyard appeared in only one Test against the 1955 South Africans, taking two wickets for 78 from forty-seven overs, and injury restricted his first-class opportunities. His eighty-five wickets were taken at the miserly cost of 13.01, though, and he again headed the averages. He also managed just one appearance in 1956, when the Australians toured, with two wickets for 49, and he failed to reach the 100-wicket mark with Yorkshire. He had ninety-four at 16.44 and that figure declined to sixty at 21.70 in 1957, when he still gave the county double value for money by taking the new ball before reverting to his highly personalised version of offspin.

His last season of 1958 brought him a mere twenty-two wickets, although they cost only 16.70 runs each, and Yorkshire released him. 'The decision was really mutual,' he stresses. 'The county had suffered a poor season in finishing eleventh in the championship and it was not all that easy to be a member of the playing staff. I increasingly found the first-class circuit demanding as we played twenty-eight championship matches. My form was reasonable enough, but I had been worried by muscle trouble which affected my arm and shoulder and prevented me bowling properly at times. I didn't want to make anything of it publicly because when I was recovering from tuberculosis the doctors set me up as an example to others. I suppose they were able to encourage sufferers by pointing out that I had recovered and gone on to play for England. I felt that I would be letting a lot of people down if I started talking about being tired or about having aches and pains in my shoulder. I enjoyed cricket, but I knew I could turn my attentions to other things.'

Appleyard did become a successful businessman,

eventually joining the Yorkshire committee to emerge as the driving force behind the establishing of a Cricket Academy at Bardford's Park Avenue ground which had fallen into disrepair after losing its place on the first-class fixture list.

CAREER DETAILS

FOR ENGLAND (1954-56)

Appleyard appeared in nine Tests. He scored 51 runs for an average of 17. He claimed 31 wickets for an average of 17.87, his best return being 5-51 against Pakistan in 1954.

FOR YORKSHIRE (1950-58)

Appleyard completed 78 innings for Yorkshire, scoring 679 runs for an average of 8.70. He took 637 wickets for an average of 15.40. He claimed 100 wickets in a season on three occasions, his best being 200 in 1951. His outstanding bowling performance was eight for 76 against Leicestershire in 1951.

CHAPTER SIX

Ray Illingworth

Ray Illingworth has had a unique association with Yorkshire, being the only capped cricketer to play for the county, leave to serve the interests of another club and return. At the same time he is also painfully aware that he is alone in being sacked twice, a remarkable state of affairs in view of his enormous contribution towards the well-being of the White Rose.

He was firmly established as the best day-in, day-out all-rounder on the first-class circuit in June 1968, when he submitted a written request for a three-year contract. Ted Lester, a former hard-hitting batsman and long-time Yorkshire scorer, reflects the widely held view when he confirms: 'There was never a day when you thought that Illingworth ought to win the match as an offspinner that he failed. His consistency was taken for granted and he also made runs when they were most needed.' As the man who has seen more Yorkshire cricket than anyone since the war, Lester's opinion carries a lot of weight.

Illingworth himself felt he had a good case. 'I didn't think I was asking for anything unreasonable,' he says. 'At thirty-six I reckoned I had quite a few good years left in me and I had no reason to suppose that Yorkshire would not keep renewing my annual contract. There was more to it than that, though, and with a wife and family, I wanted a bit of security. I had taken 101 wickets in the previous season and ended that summer fourth in the national averages with 131 wickets at 14.36 runs each. I knew, however, that Geoff Cope was pushing for a place as the offspinner and that some people on the committee would be happy enough to see the back of me.

'Unfortunately my letter did not go before the committee. Brian Sellers, the cricket chairman, dealt with the matter himself in a few minutes. The message came back loud and clear. I could go and take any other bugger who was not happy with me.'

The extent of Yorkshire's loss can be gauged by the rise of Leicestershire, a struggling county with no honours to their credit. Mike Turner, their ambitious secretary-manager, persuaded Illingworth to take charge of cricket at Grace Road as captain in 1969 with spectacular results. Illingworth's move to Leicester coincided with his elevation to the England captaincy against the West Indies, and the two events have been inextricably linked in the minds of cricket followers. He says, however: 'I asked the selectors about this point. They told me that they had me in mind as captain anyway and that I would have got the job against the West Indies had I still been with Yorkshire playing under Brian Close.

'Even so, my leaving Yorkshire turned out to be a very good thing, a blessing in disguise, and I probably started the movement towards more progressive thinking. After I had left, one or two others disappeared from the scene and Yorkshire found themselves in trouble. I probably made things more right for Yorkshire off the field than they had ever been, but then they hadn't a side.'

Illingworth's involvement on the international scene meant that he had to leave Leicestershire in other hands, a situation which delayed the harvesting of his labours. Signs of things to come appeared in 1971, when they climbed from fifteenth to fifth in the championship, and the following season they beat Yorkshire in the Benson and Hedges Cup to register their first success. The John Player League title followed in 1974 and the championship and another Benson and Hedges

Right on the spot. Ray Illingworth never bowled a single delivery without some purpose and he is clearly very interested in noting how this one behaved in the nets at Headingley.

Cup in 1975. Leicestershire topped the John Player League again in 1977, and, under Illingworth's guidance, they were transformed into as good a side as there was on the county circuit.

In stark contrast, Yorkshire struggled in a mess very much of their own making. The committee, having steadfastly refused to acknowledge any need for change, finally admitted that they could no longer cope on a part-time basis with a full-time crisis, swallowed what was left of their pride and secretly contacted Illingworth. 'Their approach came out of the blue and took me entirely by surprise, but when their general committee chairman Michael Crawford, telephoned to see how I felt about returning, the prospect of becoming their manager interested me.'

There were some complications, not the least being that the confidential nature of the negotiations upset Turner, and Yorkshire in any case had to wait until 1979 before getting their man. 'We did things by the book and there was no way that I would have let down Leicestershire,' says Illingworth. 'I fulfilled my contract with them to the letter, but, with the benefit of hindsight, I wish I had returned to Yorkshire as a player rather than just as manager.

'The original offer had been to take over as manager, but as I tackled that job I discovered that there was only so much I could do from the sidelines. Yorkshire had mentioned to Leicestershire the question of my being released as a player, but did not pursue the matter when they met with some objections. In the end, I did take over the captaincy and resume playing at the age of fifty, but over three years were wasted.'

Illingworth would, of course, have assumed the captaincy immediately had he returned to Yorkshire in an active role, but he continues resolutely to deny Geoff Boycott's claim that he had a hand in the latter's sacking from the leadership at the end of the 1978 season, when John Hampshire took over.

'That decision was taken while I was still with Leicestershire,' insists Illingworth. 'The committee did not involve me in any discussions on the subject beyond seeking confirmation that I was prepared to work with any captain they might choose. When the row broke over Boycott's removal from office I did check with Cope as to the feeling in the dressing room. He was the players' representative and he told me that not one was opposed to a change. That was good enough for me, but I certainly did not tell the committee that Boycott had to go.'

Over the years a sort of uneasy alliance formed between the two principal figures in Yorkshire cricket. Whatever their differences, each respected the other's ability and knowledge so that even as the arguments were going on around them they could be seen in earnest conversation. 'I have never had any doubts about Geoff's ability as a player or about his understanding of the game,' says Illingworth. 'He always needed to be reassured, though. I lost count of the times I had to tell him how good a batsman he was, and that surprising lack of self-confidence proved a handicap. He always had to prove something to himself and to others.'

Ironically, Illingworth's decision to omit Boycott from his Sunday League plans because of his age brought matters to another well-publicised head at Scarborough in 1981. Boycott made his own views well known on television and the manager suspended him for two championship matches. In those turbulent circumstances, it was difficult to imagine that two years later Illingworth, as captain, and Boycott, as a key figure with both bat and ball, would be celebrating the county's first major trophy in fourteen years — the Sunday League title. Illingworth emerged from retirement as Chris Old, the successor to the unsuccessful Hampshire, failed to live up to official expectations in 1982.

He tiptoed back onto the field in an inconsequential one-day fixture against Zimbabwe at Sheffield, a low-profile test run to see how his body would stand up to stresses and strains. 'I had kept reasonably fit by bowling in the nets a lot, but actually playing again on a regular basis represented something entirely different,' he recalls. 'Obviously I had missed being out in the middle and I suffered a good deal of frustration when things went wrong and I couldn't do anything about it. I got through that Sheffield trial well enough for me to tell the committee that, if they wanted to take the gamble, I was ready to play my part.'

He did this to a notable degree in the Sunday League in 1983, taking twenty wickets for 259 runs from seventy-six overs. Boycott contributed 340 runs and four wickets for 120 runs to the triumph, although in his case the importance of his bowling figures concerned largely economy. 'Geoff did a fine job and kept his nerve when bowling under pressure as I expected him to,' acknowledges Illingworth, who could, however, do little about Yorkshire slumping to seventeenth and last place in the championship for the first time in their history. 'Our bowling was not good enough,' he concedes. 'Phil Carrick was the leading wicket-taker with sixty-two, but no one bowled consistently well and the seamers proved particularly disappointing.'

This situation brought about his downfall for the second time. Working on the theory that 'we can sink no lower', the committee sacked Boycott, made David Bairstow captain and pushed Illingworth into the background. They thus managed to humiliate two of their best cricketers, for, not long before they acted, Illingworth had indicated his intentions of tackling another season. Predictably, the members rose up in arms on Boycott's behalf and voted the committee out of office, thus making way for a new regime which promptly got off on the wrong foot by sacking Illingworth altogether.

'Boycott had been elected to the committee by then and I imagine that he had a hand in my going,' says Illingworth. 'Possibly he thought he was getting his revenge over the captaincy, but if so he picked on the wrong man.' As Oscar Wilde might well have indicated, to lose a man of Illingworth's stature once could be regarded as ill fortune. To lose him twice smacked of carelessness.

'I suppose at the time I felt a little disappointed in one way, because Yorkshire cricket suffered,' he says, 'but, frankly, I had had enough of the Boycott faction, the members and so-called supporters who put one man above the club and all the other people in it. My wife and family were abused and the situation got completely out of control. All right, I don't think it was all Boycott's fault, but he certainly acted as a focal point for some fools who dragged Yorkshire cricket in the gutter.

'During the late 1980s, Leicestershire put out some feelers and eventually asked me to be their manager. Again I was tempted, but it would have meant living in Leicester for at least part of the year and I couldn't face that, having done it for so long before, so I turned them down.'

It has been suggested in many 'informed quarters' that Illingworth fell some way below being a great player and that his expertise in the finer points of the game compensated for a lack of instinctive skill. It is much the same label that is stuck on Boycott. They are both regarded as 'made players', whatever that means. All the same, only Wilfred Rhodes, probably the greatest cricketer of all time, and George Hirst, another candidate for that distinction, stand above Illingworth in the Yorkshire rankings. No one else can match the all-round substance of his 14,986 runs and 1,431 wickets, so in the context of county cricket, Illingworth is definitely exceptional.

He displayed above-average ability from the earliest days. He merited a place in the Pudsey St Lawrence third team at the age of eleven and graduated to Farsley's second team at thirteen. Two years further along the road he commanded selection for the senior side in an era when no concessions were made to youth. League cricket in Yorkshire has always been a hard school, with the weak going to the wall, so the young Illingworth received no favours. As a seventeen-year-old Illingworth scored 148 for Farsley in the Priestley Cup-tie with Pudsey. 'As a teenager, I was a bit on the slender side and, outside cricket, not very mature. Those cup games went on for several nights, attracting up to 3,000 spectators, so the atmosphere was very tense, and I often wonder just how much that big innings in those circumstances did for me,' he says.

It is one of the facts of cricket that most spin bowlers begin life as seamers, and Illingworth was no exception. Primarily a batsman, he bowled medium-pace seamers to useful effect, only occasionally experimenting with spin. The thought of extending the range of his bowling gradually took shape, the idea having been planted in his mind by a junior school master who, noticing the youthful Illingworth could cope well enough with the efforts of his contemporaries, tried him out with the mysteries of leg-breaks and googlies. 'As I grew up, I would occasionally slip in an offbreak among my normal deliveries,' he says. 'One night during net practice at Farsley, I bowled a bit of offspin more or less for fun and one of the well-established players suddenly told me, "If you can spin the ball that much you should forget about bowling medium pace." That gave me some encouragement and I got more in a Bradford League game against Saltaire.

'Playing on a rain-affected pitch, we were bowled out for about 80. I concentrated on offspinners then and took five for five as Farsley won comfortably. When I came out of the forces in 1953, Bob Appleyard couldn't play because of illness and Brian Close had smashed his knee in a car crash, so I had the opportunity to bowl offspin for Yorkshire.' Illingworth also took a lot of pressure off himself by making sufficient runs to guarantee selection as a batsman. Indeed, Yorkshire have rarely had a more reliable man in the middle order and many of his bigger innings did much to prevent complete collapse, turning probable defeat into unlikely victory.

He announced his arrival on the county scene with an innings of tremendous character on his debut against Hampshire at Headingley in August 1951. Yorkshire lost four wickets cheaply before Illingworth stood firm and scored 56 in the course of a crucial 96-run partnership with his captain, Norman Yardley. The first of his fourteen first-class centuries came at Hull in 1953 and set the pattern for much that followed. Yorkshire were 104 for five when Illingworth once more joined Yardley to add 146. Wicketkeeper Don Brennan shared in a stand worth 115 and Illingworth finished unbeaten on 146, a score he went on to exceed only twice.

He had four centuries in 1959, his most prolific summer in

Ray Illingworth demonstrates the forward defensive stroke to perfection at Bradford Park Avenue, with the famous old stand which separated the cricket and football fields in the background.

that sense, and the most important amounted to 122 at Sussex, the end-of-season game in which Yorkshire completed one of the most incredible championship triumphs. Yorkshire had to win to take the title and Sussex, happy merely to deny them, took a long time to inch their way to 210 in the first innings. When Yorkshire, trying to make up lost time, slumped to 81 for five, their prospects were distinctively gloomy. Illingworth shouldered responsibility for reshaping the contest, well supported by the tail, and his century ensured his side a crucial 97-run lead.

He then filled a leading role as the attack toiled deep into the third day, steadily working their way through the Sussex resistance, well aware that captain Robin Marlar had no intention of declaring at any stage. The final calculations left Yorkshire to make 215 in 103 minutes, a target which Illingworth accepts was 'a very tall order'. Left-handed opener Bryan Stott hit the first ball for six, however, and, as Illingworth remembers, 'the batsmen were inspired, with Stott and Doug Padgett in scintillating form. Brian Bolus and I got to the wicket to see us home and I like to think that my first-innings century put us in a position to win.'

Illingworth performed the double — 1,000 runs and 100 wickets — six times — 1957, '59, '60, '61, '62 and '64 — his best season being arguably 1962, when he scored 1,612 runs for an average of 34.29 and took 117 wickets at 19.45. In that golden summer he was credited with three centuries and eight half-centuries and with five wickets in an innings eight times.

'As a youngster I was advised to concentrate on my batting,' he says, 'but I always liked the idea of having two strings to my bow. I reasoned that if I batted and bowled I would have a double chance of being picked and I'm sure that it's easier for a young player to make his way if he can do a bit of both. A batsman who is out of form and luck has only limited opportunities to press his claims. Much the same thinking lay behind my decision to concentrate on spin. To bowl medium pace successfully in county cricket, you have to be very good, someone like Tom Cartwright. I knew I could spin the ball, so I made every effort to improve in that direction. There have always been more medium-paced seamers than out and out pacemen or spinners.'

With the growth of one-day cricket, versatility is even more important. Batsmen who can bowl tidily and bowlers who can chip in with vital runs are much in demand. Illingworth is, incidentally, the last player to do the double for Yorkshire, and the way the game is going it is very unlikely that anyone in the future will challenge for that honour.

The other side of the all-rounder coin is the undoubted fact that some players who bat and bowl with generally admired realiability in the championship are never quite good enough at either to become regular Test cricketers. Test match all-rounders are very scarce and Ian Botham is an exception to a general rule. Usually, one 'arm' of the game is stronger than the other. Illingworth appeared sixty-one times for England, yet until he took over the captaincy he could never be regarded as an automatic choice. This is not so much to say that he fell below Test match standards, but rather that the selectors felt that another offspinner might just be better.

His 122 Test wickets cost 31.20 runs each and he averaged 23.24 with the bat, figures which put him in the good rather than outstanding category, but there is no doubt that as a captain he stands shoulder to shoulder with the best, and probably only Richie Benaud, who led Australia with such flair and commonsense, is his equal in modern times.

Illingworth captained England in thirty-one Tests, winning twelve, losing five and drawing fourteen which is pretty good when it is taken into account that six of those matches were against the West Indies, who were already in the late 1960s and early '70s establishing their claims as world champions.

Illingworth is, in fact, the last man to lead England to a series victory over the West Indies, the margin being 2-0 in 1969, since when England have won only two out of forty-two games.

That season was the first in which he took charge, his promotion, in part at least, coming because Colin Cowdrey had snapped an Achilles tendon. His appointment was for the first Test only, a situation which put him immediately on trial, and he can afford to smile now when he reflects: 'I never did get the job for a full five-Test home series. I got one, two or three Tests at a time, so there was always a hint that things might change. He celebrated by scoring the first of his two Test match centuries against West Indies, his 113 in the second game at Lord's going a long way towards guaranteeing a draw.

He regards the third Test in 1969 at Headingley as his best as England captain. 'It turned out to be a very finely balanced contest on a pitch that got better as the game wore on,' he explains. 'They required 303 to win the fourth innings and made threatening progress. The important thing for us was to prevent Gary Sobers getting going and we had set a trap for him successfully in the first Test and again in the first innings at Leeds. This involved Barry Knight bowling a very wide half-volley to tempt him. Twice he had edged to Phil Sharpe at slip, but on the third occasion, probably trying to make sure he beat me at my own game, he got too far across and nudged the ball into his stumps from an inside edge. Throughout, all the things we had planned came off and I got a tremendous sense of satisfaction from that victory.'

Illingworth's most acclaimed moment came in Australia during the winter of 1970-71, when, despite all manner of difficulties, he organised a 2-0 Ashes victory. In many ways it was far from a happy tour, with the captain not exactly enjoying good relations with the manager David Clark and his vice-captain Cowdrey, both from Kent and both, presumably, with different views on how things should have been done.

A major controversy broke over Illingworth's head in the last Test at Sydney, where England were defending a 1-0 lead. Sussex fast bowler John Snow hit Australian batsman Terry Jenner on the head with a short delivery rather than a bouncer. Umpire Lou Rowan over-reacted and issued a public warning which prompted a barrage of cans and bottles and an attempt by an over-excited spectator to get hold of Snow when he moved down to fine-leg to field after completing the over. The England players sat down while the authorities had the missiles removed, but when a second wave of trouble swept around the ground Illingworth led his team to the dressing room.

His actions provoked a fierce argument, with England being informed at one point that they would forfeit the game if they did not get back out in the middle. Illingworth, however, stuck to his guns, demanding that a public announcement be made informing the spectators that unless they settled down there would be no more play. 'I was adamant that I would not let my players be targets for drunks and hooligans throwing cans and bottles,' he says. 'I thought then and still think now that I was perfectly justified and I was ready to lose the Test rather than risk any serious injury. The crazy thing was that the umpires said they could see nothing wrong, although bottles and cans were flying through the air. The one thing that really pleased me was that four former Australian captains, working as journalists, all wrote that I had been right.'

Like most Yorkshire cricketers of his generaton, Illingworth remained a keen student of the game throughout his career and based his captaincy on careful study of not only the conditions but also of the opposition. 'In all the years I played for Yorkshire, I do not recall one day when we went on to the field without a plan of campaign. We knew the strengths and weaknesses of the other sides and every move we made had a purpose. I suppose being an all-rounder helped me as a captain because I could look at things through the eyes of a batsman and a bowler.

'A good captain has to be many things — a good communicator, a strong personality and a man of patience and understanding. He also has to have limitless concentration because he has to think for everyone else in the field. Slackness can creep in if the captain is not on top of his job and bowlers are not by any means the best judges of when they should be bowling.

'Bob Appleyard was an example of a man who wanted to bowl all the time. Others like to stay in the outfield when conditions are not in their favour. Captaincy can be very rewarding, however, and, like so many things in sport, you get out what you put in. There is no magic formula.'

The final verdict on Illingworth must be that he was the cricketer's cricketer, the ultimate professional, who made attention to detail a shining virtue.

CAREER DETAILS

FOR ENGLAND (1958-73)
Illingworth appeared in 61 Tests. He scored 1,836 runs for an average of 23.24 and took 122 wickets at 31.20 runs each.

FOR YORKSHIRE (1951-83)
Illingworth completed 537 innings and scored 14,986 runs for an average of 27.90. He completed 14 centuries and his highest score was 162 against the Indians in 1959. He completed 1,000 runs on five occasions, the best being 1,610 in 1962. He took 1,431 wickets at 18.73 runs each. He claimed 100 wickets in a season five times, his best being 122 in 1964. His best return was nine for 42 against Worcestershire at Worcester in 1957.

IN FIRST-CLASS CRICKET (1951-83)
Illingworth scored 23,977 runs for an average of 28.40 and took 2,031 wickets at 19.93 runs each. He hit 22 centuries.

CHAPTER SEVEN

Geoff Boycott

Geoff Boycott, the most controversial figure in the history of Yorkshire County Cricket Club, the man on whose behalf an angry membership brought down the committee in the winter revolution of 1984, played the best-remembered innings in post-war cricket. On August 11, 1977, the 36-year-old son of a miner from the pocket-sized hamlet of Fitzwilliam, near Wakefield, stopped the nation as he became the first batsman to complete his one hundredth century in a Test match. At about 6.20 in the early evening, the daily routine in households all over England was broken as people crowded around television sets to see the concluding stages of a great achievement.

The scene was, fittingly, the home ground of Headingley, with the old 'enemy', Australia, providing the opposition and a vast crowd, squeezed in behind locked gates, had gathered to witness what they reasonably believed to be the inevitable.

Boycott, recently restored to the England ranks after three years in confused exile, had celebrated his return with a century at Trent Bridge and completed another three-figure innings — his ninety-ninth — for Yorkshire against Warwickshire at Edgbaston in the championship. Many cricket followers, cool, calculating and logical in the day-to-day running of their lives, cheerfully accepted that he had stage-managed the whole business to prove his point in the Leeds Test. 'It is quite remarkable,' he observed at the time, looking out of the dressing-room window at the packed ranks of spectators. 'They all seem to think I can score a century when I feel like it. I only wish I could, I would have made a lot more.' From the moment he marched down the familiar steps shortly before 11.30, however, there was a sense of inevitability about the proceedings. His captain, Mike Brearley, departed to the third ball from Jeff Thomson, but Boycott moved steadily along very much at his own pace.

He advanced to 34 in the pre-lunch session and added another 35 in the afternoon, the calm air of certainty being briefly disturbed. On 22 he edged Max Walker just short of slip and this escape was followed by a loud appeal for a catch at the wicket off Len Pascoe. Then Ray Bright, the tourists' left-arm spinner optimistically thought he might just have been lbw on 75, incurring the displeasure of umpire Bill Alley for his persistence. It was all wishful thinking. Partners came and went, no more than supporting actors in the principal drama. Boycott had occupied the crease and centre stage for five hours and twenty minutes when he firmly drove Australian Ian Chappell back through the gap between mid-on and the stumps to collect his fourteenth boundary and reach his century. The runs came from 232 balls and the magic of the moment was enhanced by the presence in the ground of two other Yorkshire batsmen to make one hundred centuries, Len Hutton, by then Sir Leonard, and Herbert Sutcliffe. Graham Roope, of Surrey, at the non-striker's end might just as well have been invisible for all the attention he attracted, although he did earn a lasting fame in thousands of quiz nights as the answer to the tricky question 'Who was Boycott's partner when he completed his one-hundredth 100?'

Boycott went on to 191, England amassed 436 and Australia were defeated by an innings and 85 runs. It was the first time since 1886 that England had won three Tests in a home series against Australia, but that hardly seemed to matter. 'I didn't really think it was possible that I could make a century, but the spectators did,' he says. 'They willed me to

'Stay where you are.' Geoff Boycott earned a reputation as a dangerous partner when running between the wickets, but there is no doubt about his intentions on this occasion.

succeed and I honestly felt the weight of their expectation. I was so tense I hardly slept the night before and the poor hall porter must have been really fed up of making pots of tea.'

The innings also served to illustrate Boycott's philosophy regarding Test cricket. His views, formed over many years, are unchanging. 'Test matches are won by batsmen as much as bowlers. To win, a team must score, on average, over 500 runs and when England were batting first I set myself to stay in for a couple of days if possible. I reckoned that if we got between 500 and 600, the opposition had to spend three days avoiding defeat. Brief hard-hitting innings bringing 50, 60 or even 70 runs may be entertaining and spectacular, but it's the big century or double-century which grinds the life out of the other side and sets up the batsman's team.

'I worked on the basis that with five days available there was no point in rushing. Contrary to what a lot of critics suggested, I enjoyed despatching the ball to the boundary as much as anyone, but I tried to select the correct delivery to attack. My uncle Algy taught me a very early lesson when he hammered home the simple fact that no one can score runs in the pavilion.'

Boycott's great deeds made him immensely popular with the great majority of cricket followers, especially in his native county, and his career was built on the bedrock of statistics which leave no room for argument. He was a great batsman in the true meaning of that casually over-used word, but behind the glamour of his triumphs and bitterness of the arguments which raged around him lie a number of unsolved mysteries.

Why did so many contemporary players resent him? Why did the committee make him captain and then expend so much energy undermining his position? What was the background to his appointment as Brian Close's replacement? Why did the country never give him the chance to work with team-manager Ray Illingworth? Why did they sack him as a player when he was still the most accomplished run-maker? There are no easy answers.

It is fashionable to hurl the accusation of selfishness at him, yet other outstanding Yorkshire players have, to say the least, looked after their own interests without attracting so much vicious criticism. For his part, Boycott says: 'I simply do not understand why so many people, particularly on the committee, have been so much against me. All I have ever done

Geoff Boycott in confident action clips the ball away.

is want to play cricket for Yorkshire. I was happy to become captain and always did my best, but that somehow was not good enough. There were those who found fault and pointed to an ulterior motive no matter what.'

Undoubtedly, circumstances handicapped Boycott. He would never deny that a single-minded sense of purpose dictated his life and it is a significant comment on the changing face of the game that his obsession with practice and perfection which would have been admired by previous generations earned him nothing short of ridicule at a time when the county suffered a dreadful decline.

From his earliest days, the suggestion grew that his own runs and his own safety were the key factors governing his running between the wickets, and many stories of partners being left stranded grew with the telling, yet the Yorkshire Year Books indicate that he was involved in only five run-out incidents in the second team during the period in which his unfortunate reputation took shape. 'It is stupid to say that I deliberately ran out other batsmen,' he insists. 'To do so would have been unprofessional and detrimental to the team. I suspect that in reality my record over the years is not much different to any other batsman's.'

The politics surrounding his elevation to the Yorkshire captaincy are also interesting. The county sacked Close in controversial circumstances and appointed Boycott while he was in Australia with Ray Illingworth's 1970-71 party. 'The news came as a complete surprise, I had no idea the club intended to make any change,' he said. His reaction was understandable, for Phil Sharpe, the senior professional, had been appointed vice-captain in 1970, the first man to hold such a position since 1932, when Brian Sellers served under Frank Greenwood as a clearly defined prelude to taking over in his own right.

Sharpe might have been forgiven for thinking that he stood next in line, but he soon discovered that even then the Yorkshire committee did not follow any predictable path. They overlooked Sharpe for the captaincy and sacked him as vice-captain, calling up Don Wilson, who, it later leaked out, had missed out on the top job by only one vote. In those circumstances, Boycott entered into an uneasy inheritance, life being complicated for him by his regular England calls which forced him to leave Yorkshire's destiny in other hands.

In his absence Wilson struggled to hold things together, losing his place, like Sharpe, and while Boycott prospered the

Geoff Boycott in bowling action. He always wore his cap and umpire Don Oslear has a close-up view of his action, which involved a good follow-through.

team foundered. Undoubtedly the situation provided a focal point for discontent and Boycott found himself helpless. 'I realised that some members of the side were causing trouble behind my back, but I could do little other than hope the committee would take some firm action,' he recalls. 'I thought that if I played well and tried to get everyone pulling in the same direction things would settle down, but they didn't.'

Boycott, despite missing the early matches of 1971, with a broken bone in his arm, went on to become the first English batsman to average over 100 in an English season. Previously Don Bradman, in 1938, and another Australian, Bill Johnston, in artificial circumstances, had completed the feat. Johnston, in fact, scored only 102 runs, but got through the tour in 1953 with only one dismissal. Boycott piled up 2,503 runs — 74 more than Bradman to finish on 100.12. 'It was suggested that I had spent the whole summer making sure that I got an average of 100,' he says. 'How could anyone do that? I suppose Johnston might have done, because he went in last and the whole business probably turned into a bit of a joke, but I had other things to think about. Well into the season, Herbert Sutcliffe stopped me on the steps at Bradford Park Avenue and said I could probably average 100 and right at the end I saw that he might well be right.'

Boycott actually made 124 not out in the final match of the season to place his three-figure average in the record books and his declaration at that stage left him open to attack from his detractors. It should be noted, however, that Yorkshire won by an innings and 99 runs in two days, thus ending a barren run of seventeen championship games — the longest in the county's history — without a victory. 'I am human enough to be very proud of that season,' he admits, 'but to argue that I played for myself is to ignore the facts. I desperately wanted the team to do well.' In fact, only John Hampshire topped 1,000 runs among the other batsmen and he lagged 1,079 behind Boycott without whose runs Yorkshire would have been in a terrible mess. The public responded enthusiastically to his successes and took comfort from them in the bleak years of general mediocrity, yet his stock within the club remained worryingly low.

There is no doubt that the internal politics were a factor in Boycott's decision to drop out of Test cricket in 1974, although an area of misunderstanding with Alec Bedser, the chairman of the selectors, played a part, too.

Boycott's relationships with the England hierarchy were often just as strained as those with the county committee and he still nurses a grievance over his treatment in 1967, when he became the first — and unquestionably the only — man to be dropped after scoring 246 not out. The occasion was the Headingley Test against the Indians, who, for a comparatively minor cricketing power, have figured prominently in his more troubled moments.

Boycott went into the game worried by an unusual sequence of low scores. He had completed his only 'pair' — nought in each innings — against Kent at Bradford, so he predictably took the opportunity to refind his surer touch in the face of some fairly ordinary Indian bowling. The first day brought him 106 and, although he stepped up the tempo to noticeable effect on the second with another 140 in four hours, the official axe was poised. England left him out simply because he had not scored quickly enough, victory by six wickets being no justification for his caution so far as Lord's were concerned.

The decision would be laughable today, but then it was fashionable to pay lip service to the elusive vision of 'brighter cricket.' Subsequently, batsmen such as Chris Tavare, of Kent, were to turn survival into a virtue with strokeless determination and be warmly applauded for their professionalism and commitment, so Boycott can be forgiven a wry smile at the changing circumstances. 'I will never be able to understand what happened in 1967,' he says. 'The selectors were well aware that I had not been anything like my best when they picked me. Did they expect me to throw my wicket away? What good would that have done? I played extremely well on the second day and expected them to be pleased that a key player had got back into form. I often thought back to that Test when, in the late 1980s, I heard someone like Peter May, as chairman of selectors, saying how much England needed a player who could build a long innings.'

Boycott finally disappeared from the international scene in 1982, cut down by the crossfire of violent argument over his premature return home from India and subsequent part in the unofficial tour to South Africa under the captaincy of Graham Gooch. In the third Test match at New Delhi in December 1981, he overtook Garfield Sobers' aggregate of 8,032 to become the highest run-maker in Test history, but trouble lurked just around the corner.

He had felt unwell for some time and did not really want to play in the fourth Test in Calcutta, being pressed into service to a large extent against his better judgement. As England played out the formality of a draw, Boycott, not fit enough to field, visited a local golf course. He was charged with playing golf while his team-mates were engaged in an important match, but his own version put a different slant on the incident.

'Bernard Thomas, the England physiotherapist, advised me to get some fresh air, but with so many Indians passionately interested in cricket, I couldn't just go for a walk. Had I tried to do so I would have been swamped. The golf club represented one of the few places where I could be out in the open without being bothered unduly. I ambled around two or three holes and felt a lot better for the exercise, but nobody wanted to listen to the truth. That didn't make such a good story.'

When news of the South African trip broke in February, Boycott's illness was regarded as a convenient means of giving him the time to prepare for it, but expert medical opinion supported his account. So did his track record, for not even his most vehement enemy could recall any occasion on which he had put anything before cricket. No man ever worked harder to achieve perfection. All the South African 'rebels' were banned for three years from Test cricket and while Gooch, among others, survived to pick up the threads of the 'legitimate' circuit, Boycott could find no way back.

In 1974 he returned from the West Indies as something of a national hero, having scored 99 and 112 at Port of Spain, where England won by 26 runs to square the series, and he certainly felt that he had better credentials as captain than Mike Denness, who never made the grade as a Test match batsman. Boycott, however, failed against the Indians, being dismissed cheaply for M.C.C., Yorkshire as well as in the first Test at Old Trafford.

All this disappointment added to the pressures of his benefit year, left Boycott in a misery of indecision about the best course to follow. In the end, after a lengthy discussion with Bedser which settled nothing, he dropped out of Test cricket for three years, although no one seemed entirely sure at the time as to whether he had fallen or been pushed. 'Of course I wanted to play for England, but I was keen to concentrate on

Three generations of great Yorkshire openers, Geoff Boycott, Herbert Sutcliffe and Len Hutton together at Headingley.

Yorkshire,' he explains. 'I had so much on my mind. My "touch" was not as good as I would have liked and there were some difficulties with my benefit. I thought that if I concentrated on my cricket without having to worry about Test matches I would be better off and so would Yorkshire.'

Significantly, the county's fortunes did take a welcome turn for the better in 1975 and 1976, when, with Boycott regularly available, they climbed to second and eighth after being thirteenth, tenth, fourteenth and eleventh. Boycott, in fact, took a lot of credit in 1975, although Leicestershire had sixteen points to spare in the end. Chris Old, his most effective bowler, missed seven championship engagements due to Test calls and injury and he had to rely heavily on uncapped seamers Arthur Robinson and Howard Cooper, plus spinners Geoff Cope and Phil Carrick.

Boycott's critics usually blamed him for an alleged lack of team spirit, but 1975 made rather a mess of their arguments, as did 1977. In that year Yorkshire had a remarkable run and were unbeaten in fourteen first-class fixtures, standing fifth in the table when the captain settled his differences with England and returned to the Test scene. His selection for the third game in the series with Australia at Trent Bridge was announced on July 24 at Folkestone, where Yorkshire promptly crashed by six wickets to Kent. They lost four of the next five fixtures and slumped to twelfth.

His reappearance in the England ranks coincided with the arrival on the scene of Ian Botham and he marked this great occasion with a century after running out Derek Randall and being missed at slip by Rick McCosker on 20 off Rodney Hogg. He had been at the wicket for three hours. 'I think the Randall incident was the worst in my cricketing life,' he concedes. 'I simply thought the ball had gone past Jeff Thomson, the bowler, and realised too late that it hadn't.' Randall's generous sacrifice allowed Boycott to go on and score 107 — 187 for one out in the match — to complete his rehabilitation.

The one break in Yorkshire's depressing run of defeats came at Edgbaston, where Boycott's 104 gave the first innings a solid base and represented that much-discussed 99th first-class century.

The Australian challenge on that tour was undermined by the intervention of newspaper and television magnate Kerry Packer, who, having failed to come to an agreement with the authorities over television rights bought up many of the world's best players and staged World Series Cricket as a counter-attraction to the official programme 'Down Under'. His actions divided the Australian dressing room and took such as Tony Greig, Dennis Amiss, Bob Woolmer, Alan Knott and Derek Underwood away from England. Boycott, as a matter of course, received an offer.

'When I was in Australia during the winter, I was approached by Kerry Packer and asked if I would join an international team to play against Australia,' he explained. 'I agreed to do so and shook hands on the deal. At the time I thought that they were were talking about a single series. However, when Packer's representative, Austin Robertson, delivered the contract, it was immediately clear to me that if I signed I could be forced into a situation whereby I would be in conflict with my county committee and the Test and County Cricket Board. I therefore decided that it would be impossible for me to sign the contract in that form, despite the high financial rewards proposed. On no terms would I be ready to throw overboard my responsibilities as the Yorkshire captain or the trust that had been created at all levels of Yorkshire cricket.'

Boycott completed 5,000 Test runs in the same summer as rain washed out the Oval Test, but more trouble lay just around the corner. He had the considerable satisfaction of leading England in four Tests — one against Pakistan and three in New Zealand — as deputy for the injured Brearley before being deposed as Yorkshire captain at the end of the 1978 season. Yorkshire named Illingworth as team-manager in November 1977, even though he was not due to move from Leicestershire until April 1979. In doing so, they said they had been considering the move for three or four years and general committee chairman Arthur Connell added:

'We regard Illingworth as the ideal man. We are putting alongside an experienced captain a man who has a lot of experience himself. They will work together as a team and I see no reason why they should not work together successfully. The captain's authority on the field is unchallenged. The team is his.' Yorkshire finished fourth in 1978 in the championship and there appeared to be no reason why Boycott and Illingworth should not be left to begin their association in the following summer.

Boycott had nursed doubts about the division of responsibility, but these had to a large extent been dispelled by September, when the Yorkshire committee held their captaincy meeting. The outcome was that Boycott found himself replaced by Hampshire.

This turn of events was difficult to understand, particularly as Hampshire had been censured for staging a 'go slow' at Northampton, where he registered what was widely regarded as a protest at Boycott's run rate. Illingworth had expressed publicly his faith in Boycott, saying: 'I have no fears about not getting on with Geoff. We have played together and understand each other.' Sir Kenneth Parkinson, the Yorkshire president, seeking unity, said: 'I intend to make sure that Geoff gets the support he deserves. It is clear to me that he had not had much in the past and it is not fair to ask a man to do a job unless you have faith in him.'

Every official comment indicated that the Illingworth-Boycott alliance would be given at least one year in which to revive the county's fortunes. It was not to be, and Boycott remains convinced that Illingworth privately organised the change of captaincy. 'I had put my reservations on one side and was looking forward to working with Illingworth. It was a new concept for us both, but I thought we could do a lot with the material at our disposal. As captain of England he often asked me my views and sometimes I answered the question before he asked it because our minds were on the same wavelength. He must have been responsible for my getting the sack, though. Having given him the job the committee would hardly have refused him the captain he wanted.'

Boycott played on uneasily under Illingworth's managership and the captaincy of Hampshire and, after he had failed,

The moment of triumph. Geoff Boycott signals the runs which took him to his 100th century and Australian captain Greg Chappell moves forward to offer his congratulations at Headingley in 1977.

Chris Old. There were the predictable political explosions, notably at Chelmsford in 1979, at Scarborough in 1981 and Cheltenham in 1983. The problem at Chelmsford centred on Boycott's fitness as he missed the Benson and Hedges Cup semi-final defeat at the hands of Essex. He blamed Illingworth, who claimed Boycott had been evasive about his chances of getting through the game. The row represented a lack of trust on both sides. Illingworth then suspended Boycott at

Scarborough over public criticism of the manager's Sunday League policy which involved leaving out his senior batsman, and finally the two crossed swords at Cheltenham over Boycott's rate of progress.

The angry disagreement undoubtedly contributed towards Boycott's sacking as a player, although, incredibly, he made a major contribution towards the winning of the Sunday League title, Yorkshire's first success in fourteen years. In addition to his 340 runs from ten completed innings, he bowled twenty-seven overs. 'I had not bowled a lot because of a persistent back problem but Illingworth used me in six Sunday matches. I knew he had not been happy with my batting in the championship game at Cheltenham, but he said nothing to me on the Saturday night. Next day he asked me to bowl the crucial overs towards the end of the Gloucestershire innings. "You are the only one I can trust," he told me. That sounded strange, but I did my best and had a return of none for 38 in my eight overs.'

Despite all this, Yorkshire got rid of Boycott and the members then got rid of the committee, forcing his reinstatement. The next casualty was Illingworth, dispensed with as a pro-Boycott administration took their revenge, and the club rumbled along with David Bairstow as captain. In three more years Boycott scored 4,002 championship runs for an average of 64.54, but by 1986 the political situation had become too complicated. He was sacked for a second time and there was no reprieve. His last innings ended with his being run out by Jim Love at Scarborough, somehow a symbolic finale.

The root cause of all the trouble was Boycott's dual role as player and committee representative for Wakefield. The members of that district elected him in 1984 following the vote of no confidence in the administration and they did so well aware that he intended to extend his career. Indeed, the main platform of those creating the new regime was the reinstatement of Boycott as a player, but it soon became clear that some had done little more than pay lip-service to an election manifesto. It didn't take long for the battle lines to be redrawn, with the new president Viscount Mountgarret and Brian Walsh, who became general committee chairman in 1986, being among the leading figures to oppose Boycott's position.

'The players are not happy at having a man who is in effect one of their employers in the dressing room,' insisted the anti-Boycott lobby. He saw no problems. 'I thought I could provide a link between the committee and the dressing room,' he explains. 'There was not a lot of meaningful communication between the committee and the players and I was ideally placed to do a job for the club. As ever, there were those who were looking for an ulterior motive where none existed. Interestingly, the ex-players were always expressing concern about my dual role, but they were out of touch with the dressing room. They didn't have any idea as to how the players felt. I could appreciate the thinking on both sides and explain things, but the committee wasted the chance of establishing good relationships with the senior squad. They rarely listened to anything I said.'

After dispensing with him as a player, the committee failed to make much use of his technical expertise or his wide knowledge. Occasionally the possibility of his joining the cricket sub-committee cropped up without engendering much enthusiasm among those in charge of the playing side, although Boycott made a big contribution towards England's preparations for the West Indies tour in 1990.

His vast knowledge and ability to communicate brought due recognition everywhere except on his native heath. It is in so many ways a tragedy that, in the long term, he will be remembered as much for the long years of internal strife as for the brilliance as a batsman. He never made any concessions to the unorthodox, whatever the circumstances, and he possessed the full range of attacking strokes which he employed with a studious selectivity. He was accused of not being a match winner, but he was unfortunate in that he operated for the last ten years on covered pitches which made life easier for the moderate batsman.

Boycott was unlucky in being so much better than those around him. The Yorkshire side was crammed with outstanding players over many years and, while magnificent players such as Hutton, Wardle and Trueman stood out, they did not dominate the scene to the same extent as Boycott, whose pre-eminence attracted jealousy. Above all, it is a sad comment on Yorkshire cricket that in a period of sorry decline the man who could have done most to bring about a revival should have had to spend so much time proving himself and guarding his back.

CAREER DETAILS

FOR ENGLAND (1964-1982)
Boycott appeared in 108 Tests. He scored 8,114 runs for an average of 47.72. He hit 22 centuries, his highest score of 246 not out against India. He took seven wickets for an average of 54.57.

FOR YORKSHIRE (1962-86)
Boycott completed 563 innings and scored 32,750 runs for an average of 57.85. He hit 103 centuries with a highest score of 260 not out against Essex in 1970. He completed 1,000 runs in a season 19 times, his best being 2,221 in 1971. He took 28 wickets for an average of 23.75.

IN FIRST-CLASS CRICKET (1962-86)
Boycott completed 852 innings and scored 48,426 runs for an average of 56.83. He hit 151 centuries. He took 45 wickets at 32.42 runs each.

CHAPTER EIGHT

Chris Old

Former England captain Mike Brearley believes that Christopher Middleton Old was very nearly a great Test cricketer, just lacking something in his approach. The slim, graceful all-rounder is sure now that he knows why he did not reach even greater heights for England, whom he served, nevertheless, with considerable distinction.

In fact, his major regret is that he did not realise until after his retirement in 1986 that he had been struggling with poor eyesight for a lot of his career. 'At one stage I batted in glasses and then switched to contact lenses,' he says. 'Then I developed an ulcer in one eye and I played without the lenses in Australia during the 1974-75 tour. The light out there is so bright that I experienced no difficulty in seeing the ball and I carried on when I returned to England.

'Much later, when I had stepped down from the first-class game, I missed a couple of catches one day because I lost sight of the ball and as soon as I went back to glasses I realised just how much of a self-inflicted handicap I had been operating under. It is no use thinking all the time of what might have been, but I know I was a much better batsman than a lot of people give me credit for and with either glasses or lenses I could have proved my point. It seems a bit silly now and possibly a touch of vanity crept into my thinking.'

Old, in fact, started his serious cricket as a batsman after being cast in a very subordinate role as a small boy by his elder brothers, Alan and Malcolm. They forced him as a four-year-old seeking his first game to keep wicket, refusing to allow him to bat or bowl.

He survived that restrictive introduction to develop into a fine left-handed striker of the ball, making sufficient runs to attract Yorkshire's attentions. One of the few cricketers of first-class standard to emerge from Middlesbrough, a homely outpost of the game in the North-East, he developed through Durham, North of England and then England schools. Middlesbrough recommended him to the county as a thirteen-year-old batsman and he appeared for the Colts fairly high up in the order.

In coming to Yorkshire's notice, Old followed in the footsteps of his brothers, both of whom were keen and gifted sportsmen. Alan and Chris, in fact, believe they hold a unique record in representing England at two different sports on the same day. Alan turned out to be a fine Rugby Union player who did pretty well at cricket, too. Chris, while making cricket his main preoccupation, also turned out regularly at one time for Otley as a fly-half, the position Alan filled for England.

On February 4, 1974, Chris appeared in the Test against West Indies at Port of Spain, Trinidad, while Alan did duty for England in the 16-14 defeat by Scotland at Murrayfield. Two weeks later, Chris was in Test action at Kingston, Jamaica, and Alan battled it out with Ireland at Twickenham.

'I always enjoyed Rugby and it gave me a chance to relax from cricket in the winter,' says Chris. He also remembers with some embarrassment the day in 1973 when Durham, with Alan in their jubilant ranks, became the first Minor County to beat first-class opposition in the then Gillette Cup. 'I didn't have such a good day,' he acknowledges. 'We didn't get enough runs and I failed to bowl out Durham, so I took a bit of ribbing from Alan.'

His senior debut came against Hampshire at Portsmouth in 1966, when he featured as number eight in the order and was rationed to three overs in the second innings, conceding eight runs without taking a wicket. Old's second game against Essex promised nothing special, for he batted at ten and did not get a bowl at all.

Old's first taste of the new ball came in July 1967, when Derbyshire provided the opposition at Chesterfield. He had figures of 6-3-24-2 in the second innings of a game of drifting along after both sides had topped 300 first time around. His partner on that memorable occasion was none other than Geoff Boycott, who had a return of 4-1-10-1.

Although he played several times alongside Fred Trueman, Old never shared the new ball with him. 'Tony Nicholson and Richard Hutton usually got on before me,' he recalls. 'I calculated, though, that Fred was likely to fade from the scene before too long, leaving a vacancy. There was a lot of competition among the batsmen, so I worked very hard at my bowling, well aware that John Waring and Peter Stringer were challenging for a place.' It soon became obvious that he had a natural talent and he polished it with the help of Trueman, Nicholson and wicketkeeper Jimmy Binks.

'Fred always thought as an out and out fast bowler, while Nick, one of the best swing bowlers the game has seen, taught me how to shine the ball,' he says. As a fine wicketkeeper, Binks made a tremendous contribution to Yorkshire's success through the late 1950s and '60s. He also gave the young Old an endless stream of advice. 'Jimmy never missed anything. He knew my action better than I knew it myself and he told me whenever anything went wrong. When he departed, I missed him more than anyone.'

Trueman made such an impact on Yorkshire cricket that the public looked for a successor the moment he retired in 1968. Their hopes centred on Old, whose superb action suggested that he could become a genuinely fast bowler. 'Spectators expected me to be like Fred, aggressive and hostile, but that was not really in my nature. It took me quite a while to emerge from his shadow and become a bowler in my own right.

I stopped trying to bowl really quick and concentrated on moving the ball from a good line and length.'

Once he had come to terms with what he could do best, Old established himself as a high-class representative of that peculiarly English type — the fast medium seamer, going on to earn an impressive total of forty-six England caps. Without being exactly in the forefront of England bowlers, he was relentlessly reliable and became only the second bowler to take four wickets in five balls in a Test. The first was Maurice Allom, the Surrey bowler, who included the hat-trick in his destruction of the New Zealand innings in his first appearance for England at Christchurch in the 1929-30 series.

Old broke the back of Pakistan's resistance at Edgbaston in 1978, claiming his best figures of seven for 50 along the way as England strolled to victory by an innings and 57 runs. He had been plugging away for seventy-five minutes in the afternoon session when he turned his nineteenth over into a procession. Pakistan slipped from a worrying 125 for five to a disastrous 126 for nine. Old was twice on for the hat-trick, being thwarted in the first instance by a no ball — a rarity in his case — and then by a confident defensive stroke from Liaqat Ali.

Wasim Raja edged low to wicketkeeper Bob Taylor, who did well to pluck the catch inches from the turf at full stretch, and Wasim Bari played inside an off-cutter. After the no-ball, Iqbal Qasim fell to another catch by Taylor, while Sikander Bhat, arriving in the middle in some confusion, nudged to second slip. The over, recorded as 0 w w nb w w 1, underlined the virtue of accurate bowling and inevitably Old took the Man of the Match award. 'There are days when you bowl well without luck and days when your figures make it look as though you've been unplayable. That's the way it goes,' says Old. 'I would not for a minute claim that that was my best bowling.'

Old shouldered a massive burden in the Yorkshire attack, especially after Nicholson's disappearance from the scene in

1975. 'I had to be both stock bowler and shock bowler, being asked to complete long spells on good pitches to keep the scoring rate down. I remember Fred saying that he had so many partners with the new ball, but at least there were people like Ray Illingworth and Don Wilson around. They could give him a rest, which was more than I got for most of the time.'

It is for this reason that the normally mild-mannered Old bristles with resentment at suggestions he was injury-prone. 'A few media men have made a lot out of a little,' he claims. 'I bowled a lot of overs for Yorkshire and England and took over 1,000 wickets, so I must have got on the field a lot of the time.' He had operations on both knees in 1970 and '71 and remembers those worrying days all too clearly. 'In 1976 it seemed that the only cure for persistent problems was major surgery with no real guarantee of success. They even told me I might easily finish up in a wheelchair, but I decided to take the risk. At the last minute someone suggested that an intensive course of remedial treatment might do the trick. A spell of weight training and electric impulse treatment proved pretty painful but it enabled me to keep playing cricket which was the main thing.'

Old ranks with Bill Athey and Doug Padgett among Yorkshire's best all-round fielders since the war. Agile and safe at slip, he moved speedily about the outfield, catching just about everything until a shoulder strain limited his throwing. In the circumstances, he learned to cope with nagging discomfort.

'I reckon that anyone who bowls at above medium pace for any length of time has to learn to live with aches and pains. Quick bowling is the most demanding job in sport both physically and mentally and throughout my career it amused me to read of soccer players complaining about the pressures on them. Sometimes you bowled better when you knew you had a problem because you operated within yourself. In fact, I worried about things when I arrived on a ground without a twinge of any sort because I wondered what was going to happen to me if I went flat out.'

Old is credited with a number of outstanding individual performances, the most spectacular coming at Edgbaston in 1977, when he hammered the third fastest century in first-class cricket. He reached three figures in 37 minutes — two minutes longer than Percy Fender in 1920 and Lancashire's Steve O'Shaughnessy in 1983. Old, like O'Shaughnessy, took advantage of some very friendly bowling, in his case from Eddie Hemmings, Rohan Kanhai and John Whitehouse. Warwickshire's main concern was with improving their over-rate and some balls were bowled while fieldsmen were still returning to their position after retrieving the ball.

Interestingly, he made comparatively measured progress to his first 50, which occupied twenty-eight minutes, and he says: 'Jim Love suddenly put the idea of the fastest hundred in my mind. The bowling was not so good, to say the least, but I could do no more than score as many runs as I could.' He struck six sixes and thirteen fours, his second 50 coming in nine minutes, 46 in boundaries — four fours and five sixes.

A year later, Old virtually won the Old Trafford Roses game single-handed, producing one of the best one-man displays in its long history. He claimed four wickets for 38 in twenty-one overs as Lancashire were removed for 128, and Yorkshire had carved out a slender advantage at 146 for nine when Old and Howard Cooper became associated in a decisive partnership, adding 105. Old finished unbeaten on 100 and, thus inspired, tore out five Lancashire batsmen for 47, creating the circumstances for victory by ten wickets. By this stage, he had already demonstrated his loyalty to English cricket by rejecting an approach from Kerry Packer, who wanted to involve him in his World Series Cricket in 1977.

He did not even discuss money when Tony Greig, acting as Packer's agent, telephoned him, although at that time Yorkshire had not announced a decision to award him a benefit in 1979. 'I simply wanted to go on playing for Yorkshire and

Yorkshire under the new management team of Ray Illingworth and John Hampshire in 1979 were represented by (left to right): back — Peter Ingham, Howard Cooper, Steve Oldham, Graham Stevenson, Neil Hartley, Kevin Sharp; middle — Colin Johnson, Phil Carrick, Peter Whiteley, Arthur Robinson, Richard Lumb, Jim Love, Bill Athey, David Bairstow; front — Barrie Leadbeater, Geoff Boycott, Ray Illingworth, John Hampshire, Chris Old, Geoff Cope.

England as long as possible,' he explains. 'When Greig rang me there was no discussion over details. There was no point.' It is, incidentally, an interesting comment on attitudes in Yorkshire that the three representatives of the county whom Packer approached — Old, Boycott and Dickie Bird — all turned him down.

Old did go to South Africa in 1982, as did Boycott, but that was a different matter altogether and basically the 'pirate' tour registered the players' disgust at the hypocrisy which existed in so many areas. All cricketers have tended to lose patience with a political situation which limits their earning capacity while solving nothing and they find it difficult to understand why sporting links with South Africa are so frowned on when England cheerfully compete against other countries with appalling human rights records.

Certainly Old was not a political animal. He enjoyed his

cricket and liked a pint and a chat about the game in the cool of
the evening, so in one sense, he found himself ill-equipped to
take over the captaincy in 1981 in succession to John
Hampshire, whose two years in office did not bring the
expected success.

During the 1980 campaign team manager Ray Illingworth
gave both Old and opening batsman Richard Lumb chances to
show their leadership qualities. When Hampshire's removal
from office was confirmed, Illingworth initially plumped for
Lumb, who did not, however, fancy taking charge of a dressing
room which contained both Boycott and Hampshire, noted
rivals.

Old had no hesitation in accepting the invitation when it
came his way and Lumb agreed to be vice-captain. This
arrangement did not work out too well, for Old, understandably, turned to Boycott for advice from time to time and
Lumb felt left out of things. 'I didn't know at the time that
Richard had refused the captaincy,' admits Old. 'I hadn't given
much thought to being captain, although I had stood in for
Hampshire. I was quite happy to give it a go because I was
confident that I could do a good job.

'I tried very hard to steer a middle course between Boycott
and Illingworth, although that wasn't always easy, and I don't
think that overall I did a bad job. I did not have an outstanding
team to work with and I found that increasingly I was being
called before the committee to explain my actions. This did not
make much sense as the manager was at all the games. He
could easily have taken me on one side and discussed the way
we were playing on a man-to-man level. Instead, he remained
remote from me and actually sat with the cricket committee
when they held their inquisitions.

'To that extent I did not enjoy the captaincy, although I
was happy in other ways. All the players wanted me to do the
job and I put my own position on the line looking after their
interests. In fact, being a key player and thinking for others put
a heavy strain on me.'

Chris Old was blessed with a perfect action through which he maintained a remarkable accuracy.

Rain wrecked the first half of the season under Old and, as the team struggled to find a rhythm, he wrestled with injury problems. When Surrey were defeated at Harrogate, he was the only capped bowler available and when England called him up for the series with Australia, Hampshire took over the leadership again for a ten-wicket defeat at Cardiff.

Things went from bad to worse with Graham Stevenson, the only capped bowler at Trent Bridge, where Nottinghamshire won by eight wickets. The captaincy passed next to Neil Hartley in controversial circumstances. Illingworth regarded Hartley as possessing exceptional leadership qualities, but the Shipley-born batsman was uncapped and did not command a regular place on the basis of his run-making capabilities.

Hartley actually did quite well with weakened resources, but his promotion unsettled the dressing room. 'With the benefit of hindsight, I think Illy made a mistake. Neil did all right as captain, but the rest of the players did not accept the manager's decision and it affected team spirit,' Old points out. In fact, Illingworth had an eyeball-to-eyeball confrontation with one capped player who virtually refused to recognise Hartley's existence, never mind his authority.

Yorkshire's committee had got into the habit of heralding the arrival of a new era in the club's affairs with the introduction of each new captain. Old's promotion was no exception, but he had not reached the end of his first summer when plans were being made behind the scenes to replace him. Matters drifted into 1982, but then Illingworth took over, the move being officially released at Middlesbrough on June 15. The committee swept Old away with the cutting comment that they apologised for handing him a job which was clearly not his forte. 'They said I was not capable of doing the job. What they should have admitted was that I never had a chance to do the job,' complains Old.

The end of the season brought Old's sacking as a player. He learned that he had become surplus to requirements while wintering in South Africa as he coached around the Pretoria district and there is no doubt that he still feels badly let down. 'The change of captaincy came out of the blue and my dismissal as a player was a breach of faith,' he says. 'I was informed at the time that Yorkshire would be sending a letter explaining their actions, but I had been given to understand

Chris Old was a powerful striker of the ball, as he shows quite clearly here.

before I left England that I had no reason to worry about another contract. The impression was created that I had been blamed for the lack of success. I didn't let Yorkshire down and I didn't rock the boat when they brought back Illingworth, although the committee made me look something of a fool.'

Yorkshire used the line they took when getting rid of Boycott, stressing that there were young players in the wings, but eight years on they had not really replaced Old, although Arnie Sidebottom briefly gave a pale imitation, and of those who were supposedly pushing Old — Alan Ramage, Nick Taylor and Paul Jarvis — only the latter made any mark.

Old's standing in the game ensured that he did not go short of offers and, if Yorkshire thought he had 'lost a couple of yards of pace,' others did not. Glamorgan were at the front of the queue for his services, but Warwickshire signed him in the end and he moved to Edgbaston. 'I loved playing for Yorkshire, but in the end I did not have too many regrets about leaving and I had a marvellous time with Warwickshire. It got to the stage where Yorkshire was not a very healthy place in which to be playing cricket, but things were very different at Warwickshire.

'I went to Edgbaston at the same time as Norman Gifford from Worcestershire, and I had not been there very long when a member of the committee came up to me. He said: "I will not beat about the bush. I didn't want to sign you and I voted against employing both you and Norman. I did not see the point in signing a couple of players past their best, because I thought you would get in the way of our youngsters. I just want you to know that I was wrong. I think now that you have done more for Warwickshire cricket in a few months than some others have in several years. The standards you set on the field in your approach have been a marvellous example." I thought that was good and it was a pleasure to meet someone who gave you a straight story.'

As the Yorkshire revolution stumbled on, the new committee in 1984 approached Old in South Africa and attempted to attract him back to his native heath. Cricket chairman Brian Close contacted him after he had become the first player to take ten wickets in a championship match for and against Yorkshire. His haul of eleven for 99 for Warwickshire at Headingley paved the way for a victory by 191 runs, and he observed at the time: 'I have mixed feelings about this success. I am still a Yorkshireman at heart, so I didn't set out to prove a point or anything like that. As a professional cricketer I always do my best and the pitch gave me some assistance.'

In the end, Yorkshire's attempts to turn back the clock came to nothing and Old stayed on with Warwickshire, maintaining contact with the game when he called it a day as a county cricketer by becoming cricket development officer on Humberside. As is the case with so many personalities in the 1960s, '70s and '80s, Old found himself trapped in a political straight jacket, but he managed to break free often enough to reveal an outstanding talent.

CAREER DETAILS

FOR ENGLAND (1972-81)

Old appeared in 46 Tests. He scored 845 runs for an average of 14.82, and took 143 wickets at 28.11 runs each.

FOR YORKSHIRE (1966-82)

Old completed 206 innings and scored 4,785 runs for an average of 23.22. His highest score was 116 against the Indians in 1974. He took 647 wickets at 20.72. His best return was seven for 20 against Gloucestershire at Middlesbrough in 1969.

IN FIRST-CLASS CRICKET (1966-85)

Old scored 7,756 runs for an average of 20.84 and took 1,070 wickets at 23.48 runs each.

CHAPTER NINE

David Bairstow

The season of 1989 represented the worst in Yorkshire's history. A dispirited team slumped to sixteenth in the championship, failed to qualify for the quarter-finals of the Benson and Hedges Cup, lost to Surrey, the first serious opposition they encountered, in the NatWest Trophy, and finished eleventh in the Sunday League. Brian Close, as cricket chairman, confessed at Scarborough as the campaign reached a gloomy anti-climax: 'I have never seen a Yorkshire side so lacking in spirit.'

A crisis meeting was called in the worrying aftermath, with Close and several other leading officials confronting the players. This secret gathering proved an eye-opener for those in charge of Yorkshire's destinies, for they were told quite calmly that the current members of the dressing room took no particular pride in representing the county. It transpired that they regarded themselves as professionals, more or less for hire to the highest bidder — subject to contractual obligations — and that, so long as the money was acceptable, they were equally happy to play for any of the sixteen other first-class counties.

This revelation followed a letter from the captain, Phil Carrick, to the committee, suggesting that the club should break with tradition and recruit outside the geographical boundaries of the Broad Acres. There was, though, an

Up, up and away. David Bairstow hammered a lot of his runs over the cover area and on this occasion he picked up four Sunday League runs at the expense of Warwickshire.

exception to this general rule in David Bairstow, a fiercely committed Yorkshireman, who has never wavered in his firm conviction that his first loyalty is to the county of his birth. His close bond with Yorkshire cricket remained intact even in that depressing summer which also marked the low point in his own career, for on June 28 he badly damaged a finger in the NatWest Trophy clash with Scotland and spent the rest of the time gloomily contemplating a future which had become unexpectedly clouded and which effectively ended in June, 1990.

In the August, 1988, the man who stands unchallenged as Yorkshire's best wicketkeeper-batsman had been dropped for the first time in seventeen years. Following a brief period in which he contested the position as successor to Jimmy Binks with Neil Smith, later of Essex, Bairstow's importance in the scheme of things had never been questioned. His place behind the stumps against Somerset at Scarborough on August 13, 1988 went, however, to Richard Blakey and the senior

One that got away. The expression on wicketkeeper Bairstow's face registers his disappointment at missing a difficult chance.

professional departed to do duty with the second team. His response was to throw himself wholeheartedly into his cricket and he hammered an unbeaten 130 for the Colts as their Somerset counterparts were defeated by an innings at Taunton.

'Obviously I didn't like being dropped,' he admits. 'I accepted at the time that I had not been at my best, particularly with the bat, but, all the same, I felt I was being singled out and blamed for the fact that the team were not doing well, either. I suppose I could have sulked a bit, but that is not my style and never has been. I thought the only way to show the club that they were wrong was to do well for the seconds. There is only one way to play and that is to win, so I just got on with my game.'

He had been getting on with his game very successfully since 1970, when he made one of the most publicised debuts,

That's out. Derbyshire's West Indian pace bowler Michael Holding lunges for the crease in vain as David Bairstow whips off the bails to run him out.

being plucked from his examination room at Hanson Grammar School, Bradford, to play against Gloucestershire at Park Avenue as an 18-year-old while the ink was still drying on his answer paper. Permission for an early start allowed him to fulfil both his ambition and his scholarly duties, although it ended any thoughts of further academic progress. 'I didn't do well, just getting an O level pass in economics,' he recalls. 'I didn't expect to do a lot better, yet the results still came as a disappointment. They meant that so much time had been wasted, but from the moment I turned out with Yorkshire, cricket dominated my life. I took five catches in that Gloucestershire game and Noddy Pullar, the England and former Lancashire opener, gave me my first.'

Bairstow's serious involvement with cricket started at Undercliffe in the Bradford League. 'I remember keeping wicket at junior school,' he says. 'I split my finger in the first match and they wouldn't let me get behind the stumps after that. It didn't matter all that much because I fancied myself as a bit of a bowler and I quite enjoyed fielding.

'I had a bat a chap sold me for half a crown — that is twelve-and-a-half pence today — and we needed 12 to win a cup-tie when I went in. I cracked the first ball out of the ground. It just disappeared from sight never to be seen again and we won. I soon settled into wicketkeeping and got noticed, being chosen to play for MCC Schools at Lord's. Even so, I arrived in the Yorkshire team in a bit of a rush and I had to learn as I went along.

'Fortunately, there were some great players in the dressing room and Tony Nicholson, especially, taught me a lot. I stood up to him, although he did a lot with the ball at a good medium pace and he was the best bowler I kept to. He made me stand up from day one. He wanted to put the batsmen under pressure, to pin them in the crease, and he made life easy in one way by being so accurate. I got the best grounding any player could have because Nick forced me to concentrate so hard on every ball. He managed some movement all the time and I never relaxed for a second.'

To establish himself in cricket, Bairstow had to sacrifice a promising career as a footballer. Bradford City offered him terms as a fearless centre-forward and he appeared in the Football League, breaking his nose in his quest for goals. He found, like so many others, including Brian Close and Fred Trueman, great difficulty in playing both games and in October 1971 put the summer game at the head of his priorities. 'I enjoyed soccer and did not give up a contract with City easily, but I have had no reason to regret my decision,' he says.

While Bairstow's spring-heeled agility commanded admiration and respect from the day of his debut, there were some doubts about his batting which was characterised by a certain rustic approach. 'We might as well let him slog, he's lost if he tries to play properly,' observed one former Yorkshire batsman in the early 1970s, but his harsh judgement proved

Something to celebrate. Ray Illingworth (left), David Bairstow and Phil Carrick open the champagne as Geoff Boycott, Arnie Sidebottom, Neil Hartley, Simon Dennis and Graham Stevenson mark the winning of the Sunday League in 1983.

faulty. 'I worked very hard on my batting,' confirms Bairstow. 'I realised I must play a bit straighter and be more selective, but I knew I could hit the ball a long way.'

He adjusted so well to the demands of county cricket that

he topped 1,000 runs on three occasions — 1981, '83 and '85 — comfortably taking his aggregate for Yorkshire past 12,000. In comparison, Arthur Wood, who also earned something of a reputation for making runs as a wicketkeeper, completed 1,000 runs just once and retired with 8,579 to his credit. Only David Hunter (1,190 victims) and Jimmy Binks (1,044) stand above Bairstow in the list of Yorkshire 'keepers and he reached 1,000 in the final game of the 1988 season at Trent Bridge, Nottinghamshire's Paul Johnson being the reluctant accomplice.

Bairstow's greatest moment as a wicketkeeper came at Scarborough in September 1982, when he equalled the world record for catches in a match by holding eleven against Derbyshire. Arnold Long, of Surrey, and Australia's Rod Marsh share the distinction with Bairstow, who assisted in the removal of seven Derbyshire batsmen in the first innings. Only Wally Grout, for Queensland, and David East, for Essex, with eight have done better.

'A lot of the credit went to the bowlers on the day,' he modestly suggests. 'Arnie Sidebottom had six wickets. He bowled really well on a pitch that gave him some help and they kept nicking them. You can't really base an opinion on any wicketkeeper by looking at how many catches he holds. It's how many he misses that matters and I am glad to say I didn't miss anything in that game.' He also established a Yorkshire record, the previous match aggregate for a wicketkeeper being nine by Joe Hunter in 1887 and Arthur Dolphin in 1919, but he took greatest pleasure from a Yorkshire victory by six wickets. Overall, Bairstow maintained a remarkable reliability and in the various one-day competitions acted almost as an extra fieldsman, diving far to either side of the wicket to hold the most physically demanding catches.

Bairstow, not easily drawn on the relative merits of his catches and stumpings, points out: 'Generally things happen so quickly that it is impossible to say that one was better than another. Obviously some are straightforward, but one of those might be pretty good really because it could come after a long period when the ball never got past the bat. One of the most difficult things is to keep your concentration. A wicketkeeper might go for an hour or two without the hint of a chance, but if one comes he has to be ready. So far as those which require a bit of diving about go, it is more for other people to assess the merits. I react to a situation. The catch is either held or goes in the blink of an eye. I suppose my most satisfying dismissal came at Canterbury in August 1979. I stumped Asif Iqbal to claim my 600th victim. The bowler incredibly was Chris Old, who got his 500th wicket for the county with that ball. He might not have been at his quickest that day, but I think that was the only stumping off him.'

By the nature of the man and the position of number six he usually filled in the Yorkshire batting order, most of Bairstow's most important innings have been memorable for two reasons. They have invariably contained at least spells of ferocious hitting and have often been fashioned at a time of crisis. He is not a natural and instinctive hitter in the mould of his long-time colleague and friend Graham Stevenson, who experienced no apparent difficulty in walking out to the wicket to smash the first ball for six with an effortless swing of the bat.

'Stevo was something special in that way,' says Bairstow. 'I don't think I have ever come across anyone with such great timing. I like to get a quick look at the bowling and come to terms with the pace and bounce.'

No one, however, could have played better than Bairstow at Derby in May 1981. Yorkshire were obviously losing a Benson and Hedges Cup-tie which dragged through the bitter spring chill into a second day, watched reluctantly by a muffled crowd drawn to the occasion out of a sense of duty in the first instance and by the inclination to see Derbyshire triumph in the second. Chasing a target of 203, Yorkshire subsided to 123 for nine on a pitch affected by the rain which got onto it while play was in progress. Their concentration might well have been disturbed by an incident in which captain Old was bowled by Barry Wood but subsequently reinstated after consultation with Lord's because umpire Dickie Bird confirmed that Derbyshire had not had the required four men in the fielding circle under the regulation which came into force in that summer. Be that as it may, the scoreboard sagged at 64 for five when Bairstow marched out to join the fray and a difficult situation became to all intents hopeless as four more wickets crashed, particularly as last man Mark Johnson had not appeared for the county at any level.

'It didn't look good,' concedes Bairstow in a massive understatement, 'but I knew that Derbyshire had to get through some overs of spin to complete 55 and there was a very short boundary on the pavilion side. I reckoned if Mark could just hang on and if luck ran our way a bit there was a faint chance. They relaxed, thinking they had won, and that helped.' Derbyshire captain Geoff Miller made a tactical error in using his own offspin and the slow left-arm of David Steele from the wrong end, allowing Bairstow to 'hit with the tide' towards that inviting boundary, but he could never have considered the dangers that actually lurked just around the corner.

Bairstow launched a furious one-man assault on Derbyshire, dominating a partnership which yielded 80 from nine overs to such an extent that Johnson made just four. This comfortably represented a record for the competition and the wicketkeeper went on to an unbeaten 103 with nine sixes and three fours, his second 50 coming from 25 balls. One over from Steele brought 26 and the impossible turned into a matter of mere routine, Yorkshire winning with eight balls to spare.

In the previous season at Scarborough, Bairstow failed in another attempt to compensate for the failings of others higher up the order and recorded the highest first-class score by a Yorkshire wicketkeeper in the process. His side had been completely outplayed by Middlesex, who scored 391 before shooting out Yorkshire for 118 and subsequently reducing them to 181 for seven in the course of the follow-on. The club's surrender to superior forces involved offering free admission on the last day, and those holidaymakers who took advantage were rewarded with the most entertaining free show in town. Bairstow set about West Indian Wayne Daniel and South African Vincent van der Bijl to sensational purpose, hammering his way to 145.

One blow at the expense of Daniel hurtled onto the roof of the pavilion, smashing a tile which remained broken for a number of years to serve as a reminder of Bairstow's power. His runs came in 325 minutes and he also hit twenty-one boundaries, sharing in a stand of 128 with Arnie Sidebottom which, while not sufficient to prevent Yorkshire's first defeat of the campaign in their fourteenth championship engagement, at least restored some pride.

'I hate to lose at anything,' Bairstow confesses. 'Even playing tiddleywinks with my eldest son, Andrew, I try to win. There is never any chance of my standing back and letting him win. I can't do it. It used to hurt a lot when Yorkshire lost. In my early days I suppose I took defeat quite badly. I tried not to show how much I cared to the others and more often than not went for a long, brisk walk on my own. I would march along getting it out of my system and in those days I was better on my own.

'Having played for so many years on the circuit, I'm a lot more mellow, but the urge to win is still there. I honestly cannot see me just sitting back and accepting defeat so long as I have breath in my body. I remember that day at Scarborough and I really enjoyed myself. All right, we still lost, but I know that Middlesex were getting really desperate and fed up, and for a long time it was as though I was winning and they were losing.'

In less demanding circumstances, Bairstow added statistical substance to the sense of occasion in the final season at the historic Bradford Park Avenue ground in August 1985 by becoming the first Yorkshire player in seventy-five years to complete a century before lunch. There is a widely accepted difference between adding one hundred runs in the pre-lunch session and starting an innings to reach three figures. David Denton, in 1908, was the last man before Bairstow to perform the latter feat.

Among Bairstow's contemporaries, Geoff Boycott had scored 103 — 14 to 117 — before lunch on the third day of the championship fixture with Nottinghamshire at Bradford in 1983. The size of Bairstow's achievement can be measured, however, by the fact that only six other Yorkshire batsmen had completed a century before lunch — Denton four times, John Brown twice, Jim Rotherry, Billy Bates, George Hirst twice and George Ulyett. They form a small and select band.

Bairstow made his runs from 199 deliveries in ninety-four minutes of rich and inventive stroke play, his obvious enjoyment of the occasion transmitting itself to the crowd. He also scored a century in the last match at Park Avenue — 122 not out to set up victory by an innings and 24 runs against Derbyshire. That innings contrasted sharply with the 'mad dash' at Leicestershire's expense, for Bairstow had to contend with a slow pitch which allowed enough turn for Phil Carrick to take ten Derbyshire wickets for 105. He also endured considerable discomfort from a strained back, inching his way along in more than three-and-a-half hours to ensure a decisive first-innings lead.

Those two innings, although so different in many ways, characterised Bairstow, whose every mannerism bristles with instinctive aggression. He has been, by nature, a noisy wicketkeeper, a demanding focal point for the effort in the field with a non-stop flow of instruction and advice. This, added to his increasingly successful batting, made him the most popular of cricketers with the public. His jaw-jutting strut out to the middle and the purposeful pulling on of his batting gloves, attracted immediate attention, and it was this factor which dragged him unwilling into the political arena. He had generally steered well clear of all the arguments, although he

'That's out!' Paul Jarvis (left) and Arnie Sidebottom watch anxiously as David Bairstow hurls himself to his left to pluck a catch inches from the turf.

could not conceal his anger when Ray Illingworth, as manager, promoted Neil Hartley, an uncapped middle-order batsman and occasional seamer, to the captaincy.

Illingworth, too shrewd a judge to be ignored, showed great faith in Hartley's leadership qualities, making due allowance for the fact that the Bingley product did not quite command a regular place on merit. The manager experimented in 1981, which proved a troubled season in which four captains led the county. Chris Old was the official choice, but Bairstow took over when he missed a couple of Sunday League engagements. John Hampshire took charge for championship fixtures at Cardiff and Trent Bridge, and then the responsibility passed on to Hartley. Bairstow and Illingworth had a far too public debate at Scarborough on the merits of this policy and at that time the wicketkeeper indicated his willingness to 'have a go at being captain'.

His chance duly came in 1984. The committee turned to him as much because they saw security in his popularity as for his expertise as a tactician. In attempting to rid themselves of

Boycott, the cricket committee produced a three-point plan which they presented to the general committee as a 'take-it-or-leave-it' package. They linked the sacking of Boycott with the appointment of Bairstow and the demotion of Ray Illingworth, whose reward for leading the county to the Sunday League title was a hefty shove into the background.

It was all a typical piece of muddled top-level thinking which involved the removal from the centre of operations of the two most knowledgeable players on the staff. In the event, the members reinstated Boycott and a new committee dispensed with the services of Illingworth. Bairstow did his best to concentrate on the job in hand during the long, hard winter of discontent. 'I tried to make it clear all along that politics had to end at the far side of the dressing-room door,' he insists. 'My attitude was basically that whatever the committee wanted to do was up to them. I didn't take sides and my main aim was to create unity in the team. As it turned out, I had to impose my will on the dressing room with Boycott, as a member of the committee, in it. All I really wanted was for everyone to give their all for Yorkshire.'

Bairstow had rather more than politics to worry about. The position of wicketkeeper is demanding enough in its own right and very few men have attempted to add the cares of captaincy. Bob Taylor, of Derbyshire, one of the most gifted of players behind the stumps, had a brief spell in charge before settling happily back into his specialist role, and not everyone on the Yorkshire committee was happy with Bairstow.

In addition, he had Steven Rhodes, a very talented youngster, breathing down his neck. Rhodes' father, Billy, had played with Nottinghamshire in the early 1960s, and the youngster nursed understandable ambitions to make his own way in the game. He reached the stage at which second-team cricket held neither challenge nor promise as Bairstow took on the captaincy and it became clear that he would move on if he could not get a place with his native county.

As ever, the committee attempted to solve their problems

with a botched-up compromise. They asked Bairstow to continue as captain in 1985 on the understanding that he gave up keeping wicket. To underline the degree of confusion which existed, the cricket committee voted three-two on the issue. Cricket chairman Brian Close telephoned Bairstow with the news and, not surprisingly, received a firm refusal. 'I knew what was going on and felt that several people were trying to ease me out,' says Bairstow. 'The captaincy offered no security. Boycott, Hampshire, Old and Illingworth had all come and gone in a short space of time. On the other hand, I reckoned that I could hold my own with anyone as a wicketkeeper-batsman, so there was no way I was ready to give up the gloves.'

Bairstow's stance left the committee on the horns of an undignified dilemma. 'It has come to a sorry state when players are allowed to decide on what terms they will be captain,' stormed one irate member of the administration, adding: 'Yorkshire cricket is now a shambles.' Trying to paper over the cracks, two committee men put forward the name of Boycott, who, refusing to join in any silly games, continually reaffirmed his support for Bairstow.

Beaten and bewildered, the committee surrendered and by a vote of 16-3 permitted him to remain in office on his own terms, one unfortunate outcome being the departure of Rhodes to Worcestershire, where he gained international recognition. From that moment, Bairstow accepted that he was living on borrowed time. He had made some enemies, who, lacking the courage to challenge him openly, were ready to wait for a chance to take their revenge.

In the circumstances, Bairstow showed a lot of courage on behalf of the team when he hurled himself into a head-on collision with umpire Don Oslear at Trent Bridge. Oslear and his colleague, David Constant, allowed a Sunday League game with Nottinghamshire to be staged in dreadful conditions, with the home side winning a waterlogged contest reduced to ten overs a side by six wickets. Bairstow expressed his disgust in clear-cut terms, which resulted in his being called before the Test and County Cricket Board disciplinary committee and banned from four Sunday League matches, the sentence being suspended for two years.

Unquestionably Bairstow overstepped the mark in showing concern for the safety of his players, but his punishment seemed unduly severe in comparison with that handed out to Ian Botham following his much more serious confrontation with umpire Alan Whitehead in the third Test against Australia at Trent Bridge. Botham's behaviour, witnessed by a vast television audience, did far more damage to the image of cricket and stemmed largely from his own frustration. He escaped with a long-winded reprimand, the whole business leaving the impression that his standing as England's principal financial asset held sway in some quarters. The Board's statements made significant reading.

The first said: 'The committee were satisfied that Bairstow expressed public dissent following the decision of the umpires to start a ten-overs-a-side match at Trent Bridge between Yorkshire and Nottinghamshire on July 28, when Bairstow did not consider conditions were suitable for play to commence. The committee have informed Bairstow that his conduct was wholly unacceptable and brought the game into disrepute. They have stressed to Bairstow the highest standards of behaviour are expected at all times, and captains, in particular, have a special responsibility. Bairstow has apologised personally to the umpires.'

The second said: 'From the evidence of the umpires and repeated examination of a video recording, the disciplinary committee found that Ian Botham showed considerable frustration and an element of dissent amounting to misconduct on the field which the committee felt would bring the game into disrepute. Botham has been reprimanded and warned that any repetition would be likely to have serious repercussions for him.' No mention of any apology from the Somerset captain and, although he kept his thoughts wisely to himself, Bairstow certainly felt a scapegoat.

He also believes he was undervalued by the England selectors, who rationed him to four Tests and twenty-one limited overs internationals, although he did have the honour of appearing in the 1980 Centenary Test against Australia at Lord's. Going to the West Indies in 1981 apparently as first choice, he lost out to Paul Downton, featured in one Test and generally slipped out of the picture.

'Somehow I don't think my face fitted,' he admits. 'I cannot pretend I was not bitterly disappointed at being ignored so often, particularly in the one-day internationals.' He had a very good point, for over a lengthy period he stood out as the best batsman among the leading wicketkeepers.

Yorkshire finished fourteenth, eleventh and tenth in the championship under his captaincy and thirteenth, sixth and eighth in the Sunday League. His own game depended so much on his competitive instincts that he found it difficult to organise in the long term and, although he refused to admit it, he probably found leadership something of an encumbrance. At the end of the 1986 season he gave way to Carrick, the committee indicating that: 'There is no doubt Bairstow's wicket-keeping has suffered during his period of captaincy.' He did not agree: 'Some people wanted me out. It was as simple as that.'

He settled back into the role of senior professional, playing his part in the winning of the Benson and Hedges Cup in 1987, but, as cricket moved into the 1990s and he went about the business of organising a testimonial, Bairstow found himself under challenge again, this time from Richard Blakey. He was dropped again on June 20, expressing his anger in terms which put him at obvious odds with manager Steve Oldham and captain Martyn Moxon. Uncertain about what might lie ahead he could reflect on the past with justifiable pride.

CAREER DETAILS

FOR ENGLAND (1979-81)

Bairstow appeared in 4 Tests. He scored 125 runs for an average of 20.83. He held 12 catches and made 1 stumping.

FOR YORKSHIRE (1970-90)

Bairstow completed 488 innings and scored 12,985 runs for an average of 26.60. He took 6 wickets for an average 32.00 He held 905 catches and made 131 stumpings.

IN FIRST-CLASS CRICKET (1970-90)

Bairstow completed 527 innings and scored 13,933 runs for an average of 26.43. He held 957 catches and completed 138 stumpings.

CHAPTER TEN

Dickie Bird

Life could easily have become a long series of disappointments for Harold Dennis Bird had it not been for a chance remark in the Yorkshire dressing room in 1969. He had, by then, failed in his twin ambitions to become a professional soccer player and an England cricketer, so the future didn't look exactly rosy. His early intention had been to become an inside forward with a First Division club in the Football League and Wolverhampton Wanderers, Leeds United and Sheffield Wednesday were among those clubs who sent representatives to knock on his door in Barnsley, where the local club also took a keen interest.

His close friend was Tommy Taylor, who went on to play with Manchester United and England before becoming one of the victims of the Munich air crash in February 1958. 'We went to school together and played together,' said Bird. 'Our dads were miners, but we both knew from the start that we didn't want to go down the pit. All efforts were directed towards becoming sportsmen. I had a cartilage injury as a 15-year-old and that ended my hopes of doing anything as a footballer, but I enjoyed playing cricket. In fact, I feel sure I could have mixed the two games like Chris Balderstone, who once played first-class cricket and in a Football League match on the same day, and Sheffield United's Ted Hemsley, who also turned out with Worcestershire. It was not to be be, however, so I concentrated on cricket.'

A bomb scare stopped play in the 1973 Test between England and West Indies at Lord's, but umpire Dickie Bird made sure that the spectators who were moved onto the playing area did not damage the pitch.

Bird did work for the colliery for two or three years, but not at the coal face like his father. 'I saw him crawling in and out of an eighteen-inch seam and I could never have done that. He worked down the mines from the age of thirteen to sixty-five and died a short while after his retirement. I looked at his body before he was buried and he appeared an enormously strong man, but his heart and lungs had given out.' An invitation to the Yorkshire nets at the age of sixteen, therefore, represented a passport to better things, although he endured an agonising initiation.

'I had to catch three buses from Barnsley to get to Headingley,' he said. 'When I got there I was introduced to great players such as Bob Appleyard, Fred Trueman, Johnny Wardle and Len Hutton. Arthur Mitchell was the coach, a hard man who sent many a lad home in tears as he went about his business of producing top-class cricketers for Yorkshire. I don't suppose anyone has made a worse first impression because it took me about twenty minutes to hit anything with the bat. Mitchell looked me up and down and observed. "If that's all tha can do, tha needn't bother coming again." Despite his sharp tongue, I think Ticker, as they called him, rather liked me and gradually I settled down.'

It took Bird a long time to force his way into the first team, for he did not make his debut until 1956 at the age of twenty-three. 'I can't say my time with Yorkshire was all that happy,' he admitted. 'There were so many first-rate players on their books that it was very hard to get a game and, being the worrying type, I spent a few sleepless nights wondering when my chance would come.'

There is always a lot of pressure on a county batsman until he establishes himself. Runs of poor scores can afflict even the most accomplished run-makers and any failure gnawed at Bird's confidence. 'Without being boastful, I think I can honestly say I was a good batsman,' he said. 'Sound judges like Ray Illingworth have said that they don't know of many who played straighter than me, but I was a bundle of nerves.' Colleagues confirm that it was not exactly unknown for Bird to march out to the middle with his batting gloves on the wrong hands. 'While in the Colts I played professionally with Barnsley, opening with Michael Parkinson, who never reached county class but proved himself to be a useful left-hander,' said Bird. 'We also had a young lad at number six called Geoffrey Boycott, who once ran me out just short of fifty. I was marking time, though, and trying to impress the Yorkshire selectors.'

All pals together. Ian Botham has something to say to umpire Dickie Bird, who is obviously amused.

He must have thought he had broken through when he produced his career best 181 not out against Glamorgan at Bradford in May, 1959. The Welshmen, bowled out for 137 and 233, were defeated by an innings and 35 runs and Wisden records that Bird 'gave a great display of concentration and by good all-round strokes hit twenty-four 4s.' He did, in fact, give two chances during his seven-and-a-quarter hour spell at the crease — 'at 53 on the boundary to Jim Pressdee and on 102 to Bernie Hedges at mid-on.'

The county, however, made four changes for the next engagement, with Somerset at Harrogate, Bird being one of those to lose his place. 'Get thee head down, tha's in t' second team next game,' Brian Sellers the Yorkshire cricket chairman informed him. With the writing on the wall, Bird asked for his release in the following spring, was successful at the third attempt and moved south to join Leicestershire. 'It was the worst decision I made,' Bird believes. 'I scored 1,000 runs in my first season at Grace Road and received my county cap, but I never settled. Willie Watson, another exiled Yorkshireman, was captain when I arrived, but he got the sack and Maurice Hallam took over. I never got on with him. He thought he should have played for England as an opening batsman and blamed Yorkshiremen for keeping him out.'

Hallam clearly lacked sympathy for Bird, whose form steadily deteriorated as he accepted that his dreams of reaching the international stage would never be fulfilled. He enrolled on the M.C.C. advanced coaching course and passed, going on to coach with Plymouth College, a public school, and play as a professional with Paignton, for whom he scored 10,000 runs in four seasons. 'Those were very enjoyable summers,' he recalled, 'but it was not the same as playing county cricket and I missed the life on the circuit.

'My father died in 1969 and I went home to Barnsley for his funeral. While in Yorkshire I went along to Headingley to watch a match and told the lads how much I would have liked to stay in the first-class game. 'Why don't you become an umpire?' someone asked. I couldn't be certain who it was and I had never given the idea any thought, but from that moment I decided to try my luck. I wrote to Lord's and they accepted me. It was as quick and easy as that, but I still feel that if I hadn't gone along to Leeds that day I would have stayed in Devon and remained unknown.'

Not many expected him to last long. Umpiring is the most exacting of jobs, demanding total concentration for up to seven hours, with only forty minutes for luncheon and twenty

A glittering array of trophies and mementoes bears witness to Dickie Bird's success as the world's most famous umpire.

for tea and every decision looms as a potential mistake, for the margins are very fine. Surely, his contemporaries reasoned, Dickie will find it all too much. They imagined that the first lbw would produce a nervous breakdown.

'I've always worried a lot as an umpire, just as I did as a

player,' he confesses. 'I got to the Oval for my first match on May 9, 1970, at 6.30 in the morning and almost got myself arrested for breaking in, but once I get onto the field all my nerves disappear and I'm perfectly calm.'

This might not be readily apparent to the casual observer of umpire Bird in action. He adopts a stooping, vulture-like stance at the wicket and is prone to the staccato backward flight out of harm's way whenever the ball threatens to go anywhere near him. The stage whisper is regarded as his stock in trade, so that he can inform all concerned of any point he wishes to make, even if they happen to be in the next county. His mannerisms might even have jeopardised his prospects but for the overwhelming conviction among players all over the world that he is a very fine umpire, flapping arms and twitching body notwithstanding. A study full of mementoes and a bank vault stuffed with the more valuable tributes to his efficiency and impartiality bear testimony to his ability.

The great Australian pace bowler Dennis Lillee is one of the many world stars who both respect and admire Bird. 'Dickie has a genuine understanding of the people he's controlling,' he said. 'He knows when to talk with the players and when to joke and when and how to discipline them. But, above all, his ability to make the correct decision is second to none.'

For all his fame and stature, Bird had an uneasy start to his international career, for in his second Test — against West Indies at Edgbaston in 1973 — his senior colleague Arthur Fagg walked out. 'It was the most frightening moment of my life,' he recalled. 'There had never been anything like it in the history of the game and I found myself caught up in an almighty row. West Indies had been all out for 327, leaving Boycott and Dennis Amiss to launch England's reply. Early on, Boycott played forward to Keith Boyce, who was struggling with a bruised heel, and the West Indies appealed for a catch at the wicket.

'Fagg said not out and that was all that concerned me.

Before becoming an umpire, Dickie Bird established a reputation as a good coach and these boys from Penistone Grammar School were obviously keen to pick up a few tips.

Rohan Kanhai, the West Indies captain, standing at slip, quite obviously showed a lot of dissent, waving his arms about and muttering. Fagg was very upset at the close of play and I tried to calm him down. I realised from the start of my time as an umpire that I would, like everyone else, make some mistakes along the way and that the only way to avoid becoming neurotic was to forget them and get on with the job. I said as much to Fagg, who made no reply but merely packed his bags and left.

'He obviously said something to the Press, though, for next day the newspapers were full of the story of Fagg's threat to quit the game. He had helped me a lot and I wanted to help him in return, but when he got to the ground the next day he said: "I am going home. I am not taking any further part in this game. I am nearly sixty and I don't have to live with this kind of pressure. The game is changing and it is not for the better."

'He shook my hand and wished me luck, but he remained adamant that unless he received an apology from Kanhai he would not resume. Various officials made great efforts to persuade him to change his mind as the spectators streamed into the ground. Charlie Elliott, another member of the Test match panel, was asked to hurry to the Oval, but we had to start without him. I took the bowler's end and Alan Oakman, a former Sussex and England batsman, then coach at Warwickshire, stood at square leg. I took the first over and at the end of it, Fagg suddenly appeared. Apparently he had reluctantly agreed to put the interests of the game first, but he looked very strained when he reached the middle.

'At the end of what was becoming a very tedious draw, Kanhai approached Fagg and said: "No hard feelings. We have forgotten about it all now." I don't think Fagg forgot, though, and I wonder how much the pressures of umpiring contributed to his early death two years later or to the deaths of two other long-serving umpires, Frank Chester and Sid Buller at sixty-one.'

Possibly that experience stood Bird in good stead, for, having survived it, there could be little left to upset him and he coped magnificently with the pressures of officiating in the first three World Cup Finals at Lord's in 1975, 1979 and 1983, a unique distinction.

Dickie Bird looks ready to take it on the chin as boxers Herol Graham and Brian Anderson demonstrate their punching power.

He also took part in the World Cup staged in Australia in 1987 and was earmarked for his fourth final had not England qualified to meet Australia. Neutral umpires had been introduced for the first time, so Bird had to be ruled out. 'Obviously I was pleased for the England players when they fought their way through, but felt a twinge of personal regret when I had to sit and watch the final from the stands,' he said.

Neutral umpires is a subject close to Bird's heart. He argues passionately and consistently that all umpires are instinctively neutral. 'I feel it is a strength that we have umpires standing in matches involving their former counties in the championship and the various one-day competitions,' he said. 'I am very proud to be a Yorkshireman and I desperately want Yorkshire to do well, but once I get out to the middle for a cricket match I become strictly impartial. If I had to give the decision which settled Yorkshire's fate I would not worry for an instant. All I have been concerned with is being honest. I am convinced that umpires throughout the world are equally fair and unbiased.

'The only time I would worry is if I thought anything was preventing my making the correct decision. All umpires concentrate on every ball and if they make a genuine mistake they just have to get on with the next delivery. They can't put back the clock. I've heard it argued, for example, that an umpire, recognising that he should have given a batsman out, has tried to rectify that error by favouring the bowler the next time — or vice versa. I would never do anything like that. How can making another deliberate mistake do any good?'

Bird became the first umpire to take part in one hundred international matches at Lord's on Monday, May 23, 1988, when England and West Indies clashed in the third Texaco Trophy tie of the summer, and his busy annual schedule has regularly taken in trips to Sharjah for the Asian Cup. He is much in demand both as an umpire and, when he can find the time, as a coach, and more than one county cricketer has been grateful for a few words of advice. He rightly believes that cricket has been good to him. 'It has given me a good, clean living,' he acknowledges. 'My dad told me many years ago that I shouldn't smoke, shouldn't drink and shouldn't mess with women,' he said. 'I have the occasional half of beer, but that's all. The game has taken me all over the world and brought my proudest moment. That came when I received the MBE in 1986.

'I am not ashamed to say that I wept when I met the Queen on that occasion. I experienced emotions that cannot be described in words.'

In return, Bird has been fiercely loyal to his employers, the Test and County Cricket Board. Former England captain Tony Greig told him in the 1977 that he could become a very wealthy man by signing up with Kerry Packer's unofficial World Series cricket, a sort of pirate operation set up in opposition to the established game in Australia. Bird had no trouble in resisting temptation. 'I replied that he could not make me any happier,' he said. 'I could have retired after three years and lived well for the rest of my life, but I wasn't interested. To me the Packer attitude was wrong because money meant everything to him. I could never have signed one of his contracts, no matter how much money he put up. '

'I love cricket and hope to be part of it until I am well into my 60s, so long as I keep fit and well. I do a few running exercises each day to strengthen my back, which takes a lot of punishment throughout the summer, and I go back to the Yorkshire nets to get my eye in every April. If I had become involved with Packer I would have had to sacrifice a way of life which is much more important than financial rewards.'

Bird regards Test cricket as something very special. 'There is nothing in English sport to compare with it,' he claims. 'Perhaps the Olympic Games generate something of the same feeling, but they come around only once every four years.' He also has a special regard for an Australian summer. 'The thing about the Aussies is that they're great competitors. They hate to lose. I admire them for that. In many ways they are like us Yorkshiremen and that can't be bad. I have seen the Aussies on their knees losing a match, but they have gritted their teeth and won it. That is why I look forward to their visits and why I often spend a month or so in winter over there.'

As cricket entered the 1990s, concern was being expressed in many quarters about the declining standards of behaviour. Bird, however, is convinced that 'Apart from a few exceptions — and we all know who they are — cricket is still a game for gentlemen. I suppose I have noticed two developments during my time in the middle. There is far more concerted appealing. Once upon a time, only the bowler and wicketkeeper shouted with, perhaps, the slips joining in, but in recent years all the fielding have been ready to appeal.

'Also batsmen tend to hang about more and wait for the decision, even if they know they have got an edge. Still, I don't mind. The decision rests with the umpire and whatever he says is right. Some of the umpires who were retiring when I first put on the white coat warned me of batsmen who cheerfully walked when they had got a decent score but stayed put and looked vaguely about them if they were in single figures. For that reason, Freddie Jakeman, who went to Northamptonshire after leaving Yorkshire, used to shout "That's out!" when he raised the finger. He wanted to make sure there was no doubt.'

Controversy has dogged Bird's footsteps. He stood with Arthur Jepson in the famous Gillette Cup semi-final between Lancashire and Gloucestershire which finished at 9 p.m. in the dark at Old Trafford and the same pair were the first to invoke the regulations limiting field placings in the Benson and Hedges Cup.

Yorkshire's Chris Old was bowled by Derbyshire's Barry Wood at Derby in 1981 but reinstated by Bird and Jepson after a frantic telephone call to Lord's because Derbyshire had only three fielders instead of four in the circle at the time. Bird also took part in the Benson and Hedges tie between Scotland and Yorkshire at Perth in 1984, when a change in the playing conditions failed to reach either Bird or his partner, John Holder. The result was two tea intervals and a good deal of confusion.

Then there was the Headingley Test between England and West Indies in 1988. Play was delayed for fifty minutes and another lengthy hold-up followed after only two overs. The spectators were mystified as the players left the field in apparently perfect conditions. 'As usual, they blamed me,' says Bird. 'Actually I was powerless. Water was literally bubbling up along the line of the bowler's run-up at the Rugby ground end. We found out that the groundstaff had been pumping water down some drain holes on the edge of the square and the drains themselves had become blocked. I tried to explain but most people just thought I was being too particular.'

Whatever his relationship with the public on the occasions when play is suspended, Dickie Bird is a universally popular figure. He has passed the time of day with the Queen many times, met a Prime Minister or two and told the members' enclosure at Lord's to 'sit down and shurrup.' He has been something of a maverick in a game which tried to convince itself that anonymity and a clean white coat were next to Godliness, but his enthusiasm has never wavered.

He remembers once receiving a threatening letter. 'It came during a Test against West Indies and said that if I didn't give the England batsmen out I would be kidnapped and locked away until the end of the season. I didn't take it seriously, but the police kept an eye on me just in case.'

But most of his mail is flattering and he takes a lot of credit for elevating the role of the umpire to the point at which it has become a proper job rather than a means of providing former players with a bit of a living. 'Umpires are quite well paid and we can afford to stop in decent hotels these days,' he says. If he had been just a little bit more successful as a batsman, though, he might never have become an umpire. 'I suppose in a way what I thought was bad luck was really a stroke of very good fortune,' he admits.

Bird's popularity is reflected in many ways. In 1989 a researcher calculated that he had appeared on television for more than one hundred and forty hours, mostly being seen standing at the wicket. This gave him the edge in screen time over a lot of 'soap' stars. He cannot, however, bear to watch himself. 'I don't mind being in front of the cameras, but I switch off if I happen to see any highlights of the Tests or anything like that with me involved.'

He also took part in a Yorkshire Television documentary and admitted that occasionally he felt lonely. 'I have often thought it would have been nice to be married and to have a son I could teach about cricket,' he said. 'Instead, I have been married to cricket, which is fine for most of the time, but there are moments when I'm at home when I would appreciate some company.' Within hours he had received three proposals of marriage! 'The ladies were all very flattering, but I had to say ''no,'' because I'm much too set in my ways,' he confessed.

CAREER DETAILS

FOR YORKSHIRE (1956-59)

Bird completed 23 innings and scored 613 runs for an average of 26.65. He hit one century.

IN FIRST-CLASS CRICKET (1956-64)

Bird scored 3,314 runs for an average of 20.71. He scored one century. He completed 1,000 runs in a season once — in 1960, 1,028.

UMPIRING

Bird was appointed to first-class lists in 1970. Completed 100 internationals (Tests and limited-overs games) in 1988.